About the Author

For almost thirty years, lifestyle coach Stefan Smith has been pioneering tools for successful personal and corporate transformation. His passion for growth and development has led him to work with thousands of people all over the world. As co-founder of the International Association of Personal and Professional Coaches, over the years Stefan has worked with people from many different backgrounds and professions to help them develop the career they desire. Stefan's work embodies the best of transpersonal psychology, practical metaphysics, co-dependent recovery and common sense. *The 7-Day Weekend* is his first published book.

Contact Us:
stefan@the7dayweekend.com

The 7-day weekend

Jitka,

May you always live the beauty of your dreams.

Regards,
Ricardo Semler

STEFAN SMITH

The 7-day weekend

finding the work you love

SIMON & SCHUSTER
AUSTRALIA

THE 7-DAY WEEKEND
First published in Australia in 2000 by
Simon & Schuster (Australia) Pty Limited
20 Barcoo Street, East Roseville NSW 2069

A Viacom Company
Sydney New York London Toronto Tokyo Singapore

© Stefan Smith 2000

All rights reserved. No part of this publication may be reproduced, stored in a retrieval system, or transmitted, in any form or by any means, electronic, mechanical, photocopying, recording or otherwise, without the prior permission of the publisher in writing.

National Library of Australia
Cataloguing-in-Publication data

Smith, Stefan
  The 7-day weekend: finding the work you love

  ISBN 0 7318 0850 9.

  1. Job satisfaction. 2. Career changes. 3. Job vacancies.
  4. Life change events. I. Title. II. Title: Seven day weekend.

331.124

Design by Jo Waite Design
Set in 11.5 Goudy
Cover illustration by Katie Jordan
Cartoons by Peter Lewis
Printed in Australia by Griffin Press

10 9 8 7 6 5 4 3 2 1

Contents

Introduction		11
Chapter 1	Live Your Right Livelihood	18
Chapter 2	Designing and Developing the Career you Want	36
Chapter 3	The People Business	52
Chapter 4	It's Never About the Money	69
Chapter 5	A Timely Affair	85
Chapter 6	Creativity – It's More Than Arts and Crafts	96
Chapter 7	Emotional Self-Mastery	105
Chapter 8	Intimate Relationships	117
Chapter 9	More About Men – From Cro-Magnum to New Millennium	127
Chapter 10	More About Women – From Wilma Flinstone to the Goddess	136
Chapter 11	The Only Way to Get Anywhere is to Leave Where You're at Now!	144
In Closing		151
Recommended Reading		153

Acknowledgements

I thank Paul and Barbara for being angels when I needed them. Thanks too to Stacey for always holding the vision with me. Kudos to Laurie for seeing the project through. An A+ for Sandra, who helped me turn my whingeing into an art form. Gratitude to Michael and Cathy for the mango mirth. And special thanks to my clients over the years who continue to inspire me with their successes.

Introduction

In 1970 I crashed and burned after ten years of living in the fast lane of sex, drugs and rock'n'roll. While stumbling through this disorientated decade, I had somehow managed to complete a university degree and do some postgraduate work in law. I was involved in worthwhile projects, did a fair amount of community service work, taught at a public school and was involved in various businesses. At the core, I considered myself an educator with an entrepreneurial coating. When I look back on my life and its myriad pursuits, I see myself as one of the kids in the class who has done everything at least once. I believe this has provided me with the life experience to write a book – although that's certainly not the way I used to look at it.

The expectations of my family (and myself) were that I would practise law and become a fabulous success. Initially, law school seemed the logical culmination of a very long interest in law and the legal system. It wasn't long before reality set in. Buried underneath my interest in legal matters was a lifelong passion for justice and equality; however, I quickly found out at law school that law and justice often weren't on speaking terms. I would stand up in constitutional law classes and say, 'This seems to have nothing to do with the constitution,' then be told, in effect, to sit down and not rock the boat. At this time, I began working with Dr Martin Luther King and the Reverend Jesse Jackson.

Having Dr King as an inspiration and hearing him say, 'I have a dream', had a profound impact on my life. It was then that I began an earnest search for *my* dream. Soon after, I was asked to leave law school because of my civil rights activities and for generally being a persona non grata (pain in the arse). This turned out to be a blessing; what I had seen as a succession of failures I began to view as snapshots of my future 'Life Plan'.

Before my crash of 1970 I had thought my happiness was dependent on the right job, the right income, the right woman, having the right kind of body, the right car and living in the right part of town. I painfully started to find out that happiness wasn't 'out there'. This was the *beginning* of my personal growth work, and I still had a lot more research to do.

It was during my transition that I began to tinker with the Buddhist concept of 'right livelihood'. Over the years I have developed my own definition of right livelihood. It is a metaphor for 'work' which brings you fulfilment, joy, satisfaction, creativity and money. Living your right livelihood gives you permission to explore and have fun.

Often we are so invalidated very early in life that we spend a large part of the rest of it attempting to validate ourselves. Men, particularly, in Western society, and increasingly, women, get much of our validation from our jobs and income. We often get degrees, certificates and diplomas simply to validate ourselves. Usually it has nothing to do with what brings us creative rewards or self-validation. We might have 'real' jobs – i.e. jobs that determine where we will go,

Introduction

when we will go, how we will dress, who we will work with, how much we will make, what we will do – but the question is, are we being true to ourselves?

Whenever I had a 'real' job I found I never had much control over my life. I also found that what I did well, or was educated to do, often had very little to do with what I enjoyed doing most. Having this kind of job gave me a certain type of satisfaction, and it wasn't enough.

The greatest obstacle to your highest vision is departmental thinking, which is what may be keeping you from experiencing all the goodies life has to offer. Departmental thinking is a form of subdivision; we tend to mark different boxes, 'love', 'work', 'social life', 'finances', 'health', and have learnt to live life in these boxes. However, all aspects of our life really work in synergy. What I want to do is help you bring these facets into balance and harmony.

I was involved for a time with the Institute for Vocational Research, a company that designed and marketed vocational aptitude tests. When people took the tests they found out what their skills and aptitudes were. Once they had found this out, they could find the matching 'box' in the market. When these tests were administered within corporations, people were slotted into the department or function that best suited the results.

It was during this period that my interest in this area accelerated, although I personally found the whole area of vocational guidance rather curious. What I thought was particularly curious was the process of matching the ratings and scores with various job descriptions. As I continued to research, I discovered that we often attempt to match only a small fraction of all that we are. Typically, this part includes skills, aptitudes, training, education, work experience and the like. Rarely are we matched based on what we enjoy doing; this dynamic doesn't have much value in the traditional job market. When was the last time you were asked during an interview, 'What would you enjoy doing most within our company?' Of course, application forms ask you to list your hobbies and what you like doing *outside* work.

Can you imagine going for a job, and having the process described to you in this way: 'We want to employ you. The first step is for you to get really clear on what you love doing. On your second appointment we will create a position for you that includes all of these activities. During the third, and last, part of our hiring process we will discuss your salary. Of course, we always start new employees at a base pay that is a minimum of double their highest annual net income in the past. Depending on how much enjoyment we think you will have we can negotiate that figure up to two-and-a-half times. Generally speaking, in our company the more fun an employee is having, the more we pay them.'

When was the last time you had one of these interviews? Never? Well, you can have one of these interviews with yourself any time you want. Your responses to this may include: 'Nobody is going to pay me to do that!'; 'I can't make a living doing these things!'; 'If I were financially independent I would consider it'; or 'How am I going to pay my bills?' Yet people *do* design and develop careers of their dreams. If you haven't, you can begin now!

Henry Ford said, 'Above all else, the secret of success is getting ready.' This is the first step. You've been 'getting ready' all of your life, up to and including the present. We are always 'getting ready'. Following this comes the death of the old ways of doing and being. This is often when fear, worry, and confusion set in: what was, is no longer; what is going to be, remains in the future.

When considering our right livelihood we invariably give ourselves two impossible jobs at the same time. One is dealing with the fear, confusion, anxiety, worry and uncertainty about

Introduction

what's next, and the second is judging, blaming and criticising ourselves for where we are now. Either one of these is a full-time job, and together they can keep you trapped by a fair amount of inertia.

Today, more than at any other time, we are being encouraged to face our futures because of a rapidly changing job climate. Forty years ago, even twenty years ago, it wasn't uncommon for people to stay in the same job for thirty-five years: steady nine-to-five jobs with sick pay, holiday pay, profit planning and retirement benefits. Given the changing face of employment, today more people are finding themselves either in demanding full-time positions, working between fifty to sixty hours a week (perhaps even in two jobs!) to pay the bills, or unemployed. There is no guarantee of long-term employment, and this means job 'security' is a contradiction in terms. Jobs today don't necessarily guarantee a future.

Over the past thirty-five years of vocational research, I have found people sometimes don't want support when it comes to change; instead they would like a magic bullet to accomplish change instantly. Well, if there is a magic bullet, it's acceptance. Accept your situation exactly as it is now with a minimum of judgment, blame or criticism.

I have found that when we can really accept our job, or lack of a job, exactly as it is now, then the situation will shift magically. The shift happens all by itself without suffering, struggle or pain. The real power comes from the 'Land of the Present', and success is being able to live your own life in your own way – not the way friends or family, or society in general, commonly define success. And remember, it's not necessary for you to *know* more in order to *be* more.

One of the objectives of this book is to encourage you to validate yourself no matter what your current situation: whether you are confused about what you want to do, know what you want to do and don't have a clue how to go about doing it, or are unemployed. The changing employment situation internationally is a wake-up call for many of us and can actually present a golden opportunity. Whether you are suffering from job burnout, waiting for redundancy, or doing what you love yet know it's not really working, then it may be time to smell the cappuccino and order a new work life.

This book is also about finding balance and harmony in every area of your life. I call this 'having it all'.

Getting to know yourself is an ongoing journey in life. Understanding other people is necessary to succeed, and working with others gives us opportunities to learn, grow and prosper. We are forever working in the 'people business'; every dollar you have ever received, and every dollar you have ever spent, came from, or went to, another person either directly or indirectly.

Time and money are also important concerns when developing your right livelihood. Time is a function of money and money is a function of time. For example, if you work forty hours a week at $10 an hour, you take home $400 for the week. If you are working for $20 an hour you can work twenty hours in the week for the same $400. In this book I take a look at both money and time as they relate to your right livelihood.

Building your right livelihood is a creative endeavour. In this book I look at creativity and how it is more than simply arts and crafts. Following this comes a chapter on emotions; freeing up your emotions gives you the potential to use them as rocket fuel to attract your sizzling right livelihood. The last chapter is about intimate relationships, and you'll be surprised at how these affect your right livelihood. After all, every aspect of our life works in synergy.

The contents of this book can benefit anyone, whether a novice or a professional, young or old, an entrepreneur or unemployed, a man or a woman. How you use the information is up to you. The information itself is only knowledge; it's what you do with it that transforms it into wisdom. It doesn't matter what you read in this book, what you remember or what you discuss with others. What *is* vital is that you take action, remembering Henry Ford's saying that, 'I never made a mistake in my life. I only got into a lot of situations I learned a lot from.' You've already taken action by choosing to read this book.

Whether it's preparation time or action time, take comfort from knowing that there is a map for your journey and that thousands of others are doing the same thing. Over the years I have seen universal concerns, considerations, fears, frustrations and worries arise for people taking the 'cliff jump' into living their right livelihood. I've also seen people experience excitement, anticipation, empowerment and joy in taking that jump. Usually, they experience a combination of both.

The challenge is understanding that everything you need to achieve is within you right now. There are no missing pieces. There is nothing 'out there' that will make you feel complete. Simply know that at your core, in your heart of hearts, lies the pot of gold, your exquisite gift to yourself and to the rest of us.

Chapter 1
Live Your Right Livelihood

> *'Just as the great oceans have just one taste, the taste of salt, so too there is one taste fundamental to all true teachings ..., and this is the taste of freedom.'* – Buddha

It's a cliché used often enough in movies, television shows and books: a budding young artist leaves home to follow her dreams while her parents stand at the front door with the words, 'Why don't you get yourself a *real* job?' dripping from their lips. Why not, indeed!

Having a 'real' job can mean giving up control over our lives because we are being told where to go, what to do, how much we will make, who we will work with and how we should dress. 'Real' jobs are usually based on aptitude, qualifications, skill and experience, rather than on what brings us emotional rewards, allows us to express our creativity and enables us to do what we enjoy. Of course, there are exceptions to and variations on this – nothing is ever black and white. If you love doing what you do, you may not mind being told what to do, how to dress, where to go, and so on. Nevertheless, the following characteristics can be seen as typical of a 'real' job:

Training and/or education

We often need some combination of certification (degrees, diplomas), other training and work experience to meet the requirements of attaining or keeping a particular job. Often we undertake study we don't enjoy simply so we can 'get the job'.

What I am talking about here is the difference between training because it's a job requirement and training in a particular area because you love what you do. For example, if you love working outdoors and the adventure company you work for requires certain training, then study would probably be fun for you. However, if you're studying as part of a job because the job offers security, and it isn't what you really want to do, then you are forsaking your passion (if you know what it is) for the sake of a 'real' job.

Needing the money to live on

'Your luvin' gives me such a thrill but your luvin' don't pay my bills' is the chorus to a popular 1960s song. It also reflects the reality of living in this world. Are you in a 'real' job because you simply want to pay the bills or are you doing something you love? What is your *motivation*?

Doing something well

Our self-esteem is often enhanced when we know we do a job well. When we do something well others acknowledge us, and this in turn creates acknowledgement of self. It's nice to be acknowledged and complimented, and if we are feeling unworthy, acknowledgement from other people can often seem critical.

In the old days when I was really co-dependent and needed to be liked and appreciated by everyone, a typical comment made about me was, 'Stefan, hmmm. I guess he's all right.' Today, there are often two camps of people I attract; I either inspire love and loyalty, or a comment such as, 'I don't like him.' I much prefer this because it comes from looking in the mirror and liking that person – me. I am no longer attached to what others think. I have my own approval.

Having others acknowledge us doesn't mean we are doing something we really love to do.

Again, let's look at *motivation*. Is being proficient at your job enough? When you balance your proficiency in the job against other factors such as pay, travel to and from work, and your relationship with fellow workers, are you simply staying put because the job is familiar to you? Have you created a certain safety for yourself by having the job, which cushions you from having to deal with the dynamics of being different from your co-workers? Is what you are doing *well* bringing you creative and emotional rewards?

Afraid of making a change and doing something different

The I Ching (the ancient Chinese oracle) says, 'Change creates opposition in the beginning.' Your subconscious has an enormous investment in keeping you attached to what is familiar. We sometimes call this the 'comfort zone', not because it is actually comfortable. It's simply because it is familiar. The comfort zone can be replete with fear, anxiety, confusion, uncertainty, drama and scarcity. How many times have we said to ourselves after we've made a decision and taken action successfully, 'God, why did I go through all of that fear and anxiety? It was much easier than I thought it was going to be!'

Some combination of the above

If I were to distil the essence of a 'real' job, the key ingredient would be what your motivation is for doing it. A 'real' job is usually born of 'have to', 'got to', 'need to', 'supposed to', 'ought to' justifications. However, your right livelihood, which I discuss in detail below, is propelled by 'choose to', 'want to', 'love to' decisions.

Are you in a 'real' job? Try this simple exercise, called the Ben Franklin (because he used this for his decision-making process), to see your true position now. List all the reasons to stay where you are on one side of a piece of paper and all the reasons to leave where you are on the other side. Although you may really already know where you are, putting it on paper will give you more clarity.

I have found, in my own life and while working with thousands of other people, that determining and actualising your right livelihood by earning an income through doing what gives you joy, is significantly more fulfilling than holding down a 'real' job.

Right livelihood

The Buddhist concept of right livelihood is '... earning our living in ways that do not harm, deprive or exploit other people, animals and the environment' (J Snelling, *Buddhism*, Element, Brisbane, 1996). My definition of right livelihood is 'bringing your spiritual values to the workplace in a form that rewards you through joyful activity, satisfaction and money' or 'taking your passion to the marketplace'. A 'real' job usually doesn't offer such satisfaction.

I worked with someone named Mark, who was a government auditor in the United States. Over time, Mark came to loathe his job for a variety of reasons. He quit and went to massage school, thus going from one extreme to another. When we worked together, Mark discovered there had been elements of his auditing job that he did enjoy, especially accounting. Today, Mark has a successful practice doing tax returns and financial planning for health professionals. Our work together helped Mark to get clear on what he really wanted and on how to get it. Out of the extremes came the balance.

A big part of developing right livelihood is to get clear about what we actually want. The key words are *clear intention, commitment, focus, specificity, perseverance*, and *willingness to do whatever it takes*, NO MATTER WHAT.

Clear intention You are the thinker who thinks the thoughts; thoughts are things, what you think about expands. (Thoughts are things in the sense that the toothbrush you brush your teeth with was once a thought; the car you drive was a thought; the gourmet fetta, artichoke, mushroom and olive sandwich you ate for lunch started out as a thought; and so on.) Therefore, if things are working out and life is returning us joy and creativity, then it's the result of our true intentions, that is, our thoughts. And, of course, the opposite is true. If we are struggling and frustrated it's because our intention makes it that way. The trick is:

- recognising that if we are struggling and suffering it's because some part of us, usually the subconscious, intends to have it that way
- realising this without *judgment, blame* or *criticism*.

It boils down to accepting our current reality *without judgment*.

Commitment This is what transforms a promise into reality. It is the action behind our intention; it is making the time for something when there is none. Commitment gives us the power to change things. Goethe said, 'Whatever you can do, or dream you can do, begin it. Boldness has genius, power, and magic in it.' This is commitment.

Focus This is single-mindedness of purpose, not allowing ourselves to get sidetracked. When we maintain our visions and goals, and are not seriously buffeted by the winds of daily life, we are focused.

Specificity This is the quality of being specific. The more specific we are, the more the universe knows how to answer. When we are not specific, things don't show up. Not being specific is ringing up Grace Bros and saying, 'Send me something you think I'd like.' We just wouldn't do it. It's impossible to be too specific about what we want.

Perseverance This is the quality of 'keeping on keeping on'. It exists independently from education, experience and talent.

Willingness to do whatever it takes, NO MATTER WHAT This is the energy that allows us to break through a lifetime of beliefs, patterns, behaviours and emotions. This is what moves the mountains. It empowers us to 'leap tall buildings in a single bound, travel faster than a speeding bullet, be more powerful than a locomotive'.

———•———

When determining right livelihood, the first thing to do is to look at everything that is working in our present work-related scenario. No matter what our emotions or situation, more of life is working for us than isn't. In other words see the glass a bit more than half full. It's easier to build on that.

The illusion that nothing is working is often sparked because of our conditioning from family and society at large, which involves judgment, blame and criticism. We often forget to look at what is working in our lives because we are so busy focusing on what *isn't*. We are so caught up with what we *don't* have and what we *are not* that we forget about the things we *do* have. Crosby, Stills and Nash sing, 'If you can't be with the one you love, love the one you're with.' Not to love the one you're with implies, 'I will be happy when …'; 'I will be happy if …'.

I wrote a regular column called 'The Great American Business Machine' for a newspaper. Every column I wrote was a spoof on some facet of American business. I always wrote the column at the last minute, getting up at three in the morning for a 9 am deadline even though I knew months ahead when it was due. I'd huff and puff into the office at 9 am and slide over to my editor, apologising profusely. One day she told me to sit down. She said, 'You've never been late for a column and their quality is excellent. What are you doing to yourself?' She then went on to say, 'You are not procrastinating, it's just that it didn't have to be done until now.' I said, 'That's too simple!'

If you really want to be with the one you love – whether the one you love is your right livelihood, a fit and healthy physical body, a successful relationship, more money, a creative environment – begin *now* by loving the one you're with. How much of your present happiness are you sacrificing for some future condition?

If you are not clear on what you *do* want, get clear on what you *don't* want. A lot of people don't know what they want; yet, in my experience, when I ask people if they know what they don't want, they invariably reply, 'Yeah, of course.' If this really is the case then they are halfway there!

By recognising and accepting that more of our life is working than not, we create more available energy for the *transition* to the next step. This is because we are moving to the next step as part of a celebration and not primarily from a place of frustration. It takes an enormous amount of energy to avoid something, energy we could be directing elsewhere.

Moving towards your right livelihood

Right livelihood involves crossing a bridge from the old reality to the new (I discuss this in greater detail in the next chapter). Crossing that bridge can be slow and painful, quick and painful, slow and easy, or quick and easy; you have the choice. The more we can accept our present employment situation with appreciation and gratitude, the easier the transition to our right livelihood will be.

American Indians talk about the Field of Plenty: Gratitude equals Trust plus Action.' This says that whatever you want in life (and it extends to all areas of your life not simply right livelihood), give thanks for it in the present. Sometimes this may be difficult because we don't know what we are giving thanks for; however, we trust that *it is happening* in the present, not that *it will happen* in the future. The Rolling Stones sang, 'Ah cain't git no satisfaction.' The point is, unless we can find satisfaction in where we are now it doesn't matter what our external world is offering us; we won't see it.

Acceptance is the first step towards developing our right livelihood. Then comes action. The only way to get anywhere else is to leave where we are now. *Inventory* and *completion* are fundamental action steps toward creating your right livelihood.

Inventory

If we had a retail store we would have an inventory system to know when to order more of the items that are selling, when to have a sale to get rid of the items that are not selling, when to stock and when to reorder.

How often, though, and how thoroughly, do we sit down to inventory our life?

We generally have an idea of what's working and what's not working in life. As mentioned previously, specificity can be a key to the clarity we want. Actually writing down the areas gives us the realistic self-appraisal required as part of the foundation for change.

A simple way to inventory our career or present job is to take four areas of our present work situation and rate our level of satisfaction on a scale of 1–10, '10' being total satisfaction and '1' being total dissatisfaction.

The first area to inventory is time. That is, travel time (to and from work), time spent at work, time spent working at home after work and time off. For example, if it takes you thirty minutes to get to work, that's a total of about five hours per week. That may be acceptable to you, particularly if it's a fairly easy trip. You may even rate travel time at a '9' if you are in this situation.

However, if you average a forty-hour week at the office and you're not very keen on that any longer, you may be rating time spent at work as a '4'. If your job includes work at home after hours, rate your level of satisfaction with that. If you're rating a forty-hour week as a '4', chances are you're not much happier with taking work home, and are looking at giving working at home a rating of '2'. (Remember, this is an example only. Your numbers could be much higher than these; after all, it's your inventory.)

Now, you have an average of three weeks, plus public holidays, off. It's not enough for you, so you give time off a '4'.

Your average over all is a 4.75 on a scale of 1–10. You would have already known pretty much how you felt about all of this, and being specific can fix your intention in a powerful fashion. This kind of inventory is particularly helpful if you are in a different situation from that outlined above, that is, you are self-employed or in a position to plan your own schedule.

When you really think about it, time is the most valuable thing we have (more about time later on).

The second area is money. Do you feel you are being generously rewarded for the *value* and *use* of your time? Once again, ask yourself for a rating of the level of compensation you are receiving, either from employment by others or from self-employment. It's a powerful feeling to know that the investment of your time and effort is being justly rewarded. If you're not feeling that way, put that number down that reflects your level of satisfaction. Remember, even if you're giving things low ratings, it's a start in developing a map for yourself. Always begin with NOW.

The third area is the actual work you are doing. Are you being rewarded creatively? Are you being rewarded emotionally? Is what you are doing fun? You can take these three questions and rate them separately, then average them, or rate the entire area of your work satisfaction collectively. Basically, what you want show yourself is where you are now in your work. Surprisingly enough, many people find that they are actually in *better* shape regarding work than they thought. Knowing this can be empowering during transitions because you are able to look at things more clearly. The only way to get anywhere else is to leave where you are at now. The greater your clarity in the now, the easier it will be for you to get what you want in the future.

The final area is your level of satisfaction with colleagues and associates. Are the people you work with fun to play with at work? Do they support you? Do you support them? Do they say what they mean? Do they do what they say? Do you look forward to associating with them on a regular basis? Do they *add* to who you are or do they drain your energy and waste your time? Are you aligned with them or are they from some TV comedy series – only they're not funny? Are some great, and some ... and some ... well, you know? Work out an average, giving yourself a number between one and ten.

Add up your score and divide by four. If you get a score of eight or below, you undoubtedly have some dissatisfaction with your job, and now your challenge is to pinpoint the frustrations. Is it time to move on to greener pastures? Or do you want to make some changes within the job to improve your satisfaction?

Completion

Before quitting your job and rushing into your right livelihood, take time to *complete*. Completing a 'real' job means extracting skills, experiences and lessons from it, and applying them to your right livelihood. That is, you use what you already have to develop your right livelihood. Completion allows transition from one reality to another; it doesn't mean we end one reality one day, only to wake up the next day firmly entrenched in our right livelihood. Namely, you don't wake up one morning after a hot, sunny summer's day and lie shivering in bed because it's winter and snowing outside. Autumn and spring are the bridges between winter and summer; they are also the *completions* of summer and winter.

Completion is coming to a total acceptance of the way things are. If we complete a relationship, for example, we may keep the love and change the way we interact with the other person. This is different from *ending* a relationship, which implies moving on without looking back. What you want to do with your present job is to complete it, not end it. It's only in completion that you can move on to the next stage of your life without the old baggage.

Form and function

Form and function are important aspects of right livelihood. In the West we are what I call 'form-challenged'. That means we live in a society that 'grows' butchers, bakers and candlestick makers. We attempt to fit all our exquisite, multi-dimensional aspects, those that make us uniquely ourselves (function), into a job description (form). What I do with form(s) is actually create ones which fit more of who people really are.

The challenge comes when you ask people what they enjoy doing. Say it's being out in nature, swimming, painting, hanging out with people, travelling. They'll make this great list of all the things they love doing and then say, 'No one will pay me to do that!', or 'Come on, I need to support myself!' It doesn't fit a preconceived form, or job description, so it's abandoned. I then ask people to take the form, put it on the shelf for a little while and simply concentrate on what they enjoy doing. Forget about money, forget about form, forget about job description. Let's design and develop the 'job' from the ground up.

I was hanging out at my sister's place one day. She had a two-car garage and suggested I do it up as a playroom for my young nieces. I liked being creative with my hands, so I thought, 'OK, let's see what I can do.' I ended up doing some pretty wild things with different coloured carpet, placing it around the walls to make the playroom safe. The playroom ended up being quite spectacular acoustically, functionally and visually. Then one of her neighbours saw it and said, 'That's pretty neat, do you want to build a wall unit for us?' I thought that could be fun, so I agreed. I got together with a wild Argentinian sculptor and we built a $30,000 wall unit. Then another neighbour saw it and said, 'We want a tropical outdoor spa pool; can you do that?' I said, 'Sure.'

I'd never done any of these things before; I simply knew that I loved designing and creating things with my hands. However, what evolved was a business. I came up with a letterhead that read, 'Design and Building Consultants [I had never heard of this term before, I just made it up], Residential, Industrial, Commercial.'

Live Your Right Livelihood

I created what I *wanted* to do based on what I knew I *didn't* want to do. I didn't want to be a builder because I didn't want to go through the whole licensing process. I had an eye for design, yet didn't want to go back to university for four years and become an architect.

I ended up restoring turn-of-the-century vintage houses, and I had experts in the trade teach me the business. That is, I chose tradespeople who gave me what I wanted: price, quality, dependability, a happy attitude and the willingness to teach their 'boss'. It was an unusual arrangement; I gave them the work, yet they were the teachers, contradicting the notion that 'the boss usually knows more'. In a 'real' job you usually have the boss at the top and the employee at the bottom, with very little equality. I like working with everyone as equals no matter who they are.

My design and building consultancy business showed me quite powerfully that if you want to do for a living what you love to do, it's not necessary to know everything about it; if you have the passion, the knowledge will follow. I made the form fit the function rather than trying to cram the function into the form. In short, my suggestion to you is don't worry about the *form* because it will follow *function*.

I see examples of how form and function work together every day. Recently, I caught a bus from Newport, Sydney, into Central Station in the city. Halfway there the bus driver crashed into a concrete pole, taking both himself and the bus out of action. I waited twenty-five minutes for the next bus to come along, got on the bus, showed my ticket, then the driver said to me, 'We don't take transfers.' I said, 'This is not a transfer, this is the result of the last driver having smashed into that pole right there and taking himself out of service.' To this, the bus driver responded, 'Well, I didn't smash into the pole!'

I felt the bus driver obviously had an attachment to form. His *function* was to get his passenger to town – a passenger who had already paid to get to that destination. The *form* was that the bus driver was never to pick up transferred passengers. I had my own attachment to function, i.e. getting to the city on time for an appointment.

I said to the driver: 'You have these choices. First, you can call your supervisor, or, second, you can call the police, or, third, you can just take me into town. What'll it be?' He just grumbled something unintelligible and gestured for me to take a seat.

One woman who came to see me, Jo, was able to create a job she loved using the skills she already had. Jo was working for a computer company in Northern California. She hated her job, and came to me because she thought she wanted to get out of the industry and do something about developing a new career for herself. During her time with me she became clearer about what she valued, finding that she really loved working with computers. She came to know what she wanted regarding *who* she wanted to work with, *how* she wanted to work and *what* she wanted to be doing.

It wasn't long after this that Jo was hired by one of the largest computer companies in the world after they did a nationwide search for a Manager of Quality Assurance. She started to work with a whole different team, a functional team, as opposed to the dysfunctional management team she had been working with previously. The *form* of her work changed, the *function* did not.

Vocation

Right livelihood implies vocation, which comes from the Latin word *vocare* and means 'a calling'. When conflict arises it is usually because most of us know on some level that we have 'a calling', whether the language we use for it is saying 'Yes!' to the life we want, doing what we really love, right livelihood, life purpose or mission. However we say it, many of us recognise that our 'calling' is not necessarily what we are doing to make a living. That's where the conflict arises.

A 'calling' is often that wee voice in us that is whispering about a higher purpose and asking us to express ourselves emotionally and/or creatively. The trick is to hear the voice, listen to the voice and act on the voice. Typically, action-taking is fraught with confusion and fear. It's all about embracing the fear and confusion, and *fearing forward*.

Next time you're fearful, look down at your knees and see them knocking; also notice one foot being placed in front of the other, moving forward to the 'what ifs' of the future and leaving behind the 'if onlys' from the past. This is 'fearing forward'. Your power is in the *present*, and it comes when you release yourself from your own judgment, blame and criticism. Accept your feelings and emotions as part of being fully human, and move towards your goals despite your fears.

The tools

Values clarification and realistic self-appraisal are helpful tools when it comes to *fearing forward*.

What do you value?

To clarify your next step, begin with making an inventory of the ten things you enjoy doing most. Start with a list of twenty or thirty things and select the top ten. (If you find this initial part challenging, there is an important message for you right there.)

With this list write a third-person overview. For example, say your list included working with computers, being at home, being with the family, networking and working your own hours. A job to fit your list might be starting and running a home-based computer company.

Even though you know you wrote the list, pretend someone was asking you for your objective opinion of this person (you) based on what they enjoy doing most. Pretend you are a psychologist or sociologist and start writing. You may even consider going to someone else and letting them give you some feedback.

After you've done this, start recommending to yourself suitable jobs that might correspond with the list. You may not be able to find the job in a phone book, a list of vocations or the local newspaper – so just make it up. It needn't have any label on it.

I am asking you to go as far out in left field as possible – or right field, because the left brain is the logical side looking for reason and saying, 'Nobody is going to pay me any money for doing this.' What I aim to do is to help you push past the creative barrier and encourage you to let go of your attachment to form.

We are then going to see how your 'real' job relates to your right livelihood. I don't want people simply to be so sick and tired of what they do that they quit their job immediately. I'm not going to ask you to 'throw out the baby with the bathwater'. Instead, what I'm asking is that you begin to work out what your right livelihood might be and then consider the transition to it.

Realistic self-appraisal

Realistic self-appraisal (RSA) is the ability to see ourselves clearly. The influence of our beliefs and behaviours often keeps us from seeing ourselves in our true resplendent glory: that is, who we *really* are, including the *power* we have, the *creativity* we can express, and the joy and *happiness* we can have in our lives.

A simple example of RSA is how we see our physical body. A straightforward exercise is to stand naked in front of a full-length mirror and just look at who you are. You are not looking *at* certain things, or *for* certain things; you are *simply looking*. Do this three minutes three times a week for three weeks, two minutes twice a week for two weeks and one minute for one week.

RSA can be applied to any situation in life. At work, simply focus on what is happening without judging, blaming or criticising yourself, others or the situation. Take it one step further and make a list of what *is* working and what *isn't* working in your job. Again, it's about being grateful for what you have and acknowledging that in any given situation there's a great deal that *is* working successfully. In your present job, taking the time to acknowledge what *is* working and giving thanks for this is one of the most important keys to taking the next step of finding your right livelihood.

Imagist Gerard Toye said, 'The truth will set you free but it will piss you off at first.'

Chapter 2
Designing and Developing the Career you Want

'Work is love made visible' – Khalil Gibran

You know you are enjoying your sizzling right livelihood when you can't wait to get up in the morning to go to 'work'. Right livelihood is being able to express most – if not all – of ourselves creatively and emotionally. We feel physically stronger, we have more energy and those recurring headaches disappear.

Your right livelihood can be a retail business, a private practice, or a job that embodies the essence of what you really want to do. Whatever form it takes, your right livelihood is a business. In developing your right livelihood, you can begin part-time and still keep your 'real' job or you can 'cliff jump' and simply quit your old job.

If you choose the latter and plan to move towards establishing your own business, then heed this: make sure you have adequate financial reserves to cover your basic needs for two years. Ninety per cent of new businesses fail in the first year. Ninety per cent of those that remain fail in the second year. The survival rate for the remainder increases to between 90 to 95 per cent at the ten-year mark.

The primary reasons for failure of businesses are *undercapitalisation* and *mismanagement*.

Undercapitalisation

Undercapitalisation means depending on your new business to support you within the first two years of its operation. *Proper* capitalisation can mean having a part-time job to cover your basic overheads, or having sufficient initial capital so you don't rely on profit from the business.

A burgeoning new business can create a false sense of security in the first year; after six months people think they have made it because their business is thriving. Watch out for this. As with any new relationship there is usually an initial 'honeymoon' period. Establish the building blocks in the first two years of business, adapting your systems and being mindful of building a strong foundation. Life is a series of changes, and unless a firm foundation is established your business can fail even if you have experienced success with it initially.

Mismanagement

Mismanagement can occur in businesses ranging from tiny Ma and Pa bakeries to multinational, multimillion dollar companies. If we haven't had a failed business ourselves, many of us know someone who has. These businesses have left a long trail of unhappy stories behind them, even though their paths were initially paved with well-meaning intentions.

Classically, mismanagement means not keeping to the basics of business, which include marketing, management, finance and operations. Mismanagement means not knowing these systems exist – or not using them. The systems succeed if you *work* with them, and this requires knowing what you don't know about the systems.

For example, Sharon wanted to open a clothing store. She had had a lifelong love for design and making clothes and ran a small business from home. Sharon also had a full-time job which, over time, slipped into becoming a 'real' job she no longer enjoyed. Her friends and family applauded her skills and talent and encouraged her. People would often say to her, 'Why don't you open your own store?' Sharon decided to do it. She quit her job, borrowed some money and opened a store. Eleven months later Sharon sadly closed her business and went back to having a 'real' job.

Sharon had thought she would have a great time making and selling clothes; she didn't understand what was involved in running a business. She didn't have a business plan, and because she had quit her job she was relying on her new business to support her. She hadn't accounted for increased expenses such as rent, advertising, insurance, equipment, and the like. As a result, Sharon became so caught up with the administration side of her business she didn't have time to do what she really enjoyed.

Six months on she hired help so she could concentrate on designing and making clothes. However, what Sharon still didn't have was the systems. She had someone who could do the books – and no-one to advise her on marketing, management or operations (see below). This was why the business slowly crumbled.

This is a classic example of mismanagement and under-capitalisation. People who love to cook so much that everything they prepare is a culinary delight, open restaurants.

Others love to bake, so they open up a bakery, and it goes on. Simply doing what we love to do and what we are passionate about doesn't guarantee success in following our right livelihood.

Knowing basic principles

Once more, when your right livelihood involves running your own business, it is not enough simply to live your passion. As mentioned before, it's vital to follow the basic principles of business, which include marketing, management, finance and operations.

Marketing

Marketing is getting your product and/or service from where it is now to where you want it to be: that is, out into the appropriate marketplace. Marketing includes advertising, promotion, publicity and public relations. You must tell the right people about your product or service and be able to deliver it to them. You can do this by targeting your market and finding the vehicles that reach it.

Management

Management is partly your ability to develop and use an effective business plan. It is also about knowing whether it is time to work with other people – and choosing the appropriate people to work with. This means using discrimination in your choice of employees, lawyers, accountants, advisers, suppliers, consultants, landlords, bankers, partners and others.

Finance

Systems in finance include those for budgeting, accounting, banking relationships and other aspects of capitalisation. It is essential to get expert advice on these matters, primarily from an experienced accountant.

Operations

Operations are how you are running your business. That is, for example, design, décor and location of your premises, your trading hours, maintenance, telephone systems – the nuts and bolts of your business.

For more information on these systems I recommend Michael E. Gerber's book, *E-Myth Revisited*. It was written for people who think they will have more freedom when they work for themselves and then find that their business is running *them*. They have less time, less money and more stress. Anyway, for more information about the how-to's of business, visit your a bookshop or a local library, a university or business centre. You may also like to enrol in a course; government-run classes exist for the long-term unemployed.

If you are not interested in the basic elements of business, either:

- get yourself a business manager who *does* enjoy the nuts and bolts of business and has a successful track record
- employ a business adviser or consultant, or
- take a basic course in business administration.

Inner and outer change

What you want to do is to take *function*, which is finding out what your passion is, and to balance it with *form*, so you can entertain the possibility of financial independence while doing what you *really* love.

As you've seen, over the years I've witnessed people with good intentions quit their 'real' jobs and open up businesses doing what they love to do. A year later they are on unemployment benefits or looking for other 'real' jobs. I don't want this to happen to you, and that's why an understanding of how to make an orderly transition from your old reality to your new reality is important in finding your right livelihood.

Transition

Transition is the process of 'moving across'. If you see where you are right now as being on a bridge, you can look back to where you have been and get a glimpse of where you want to go. This is a powerful part of getting ready. You are on the bridge moving forward; it doesn't matter if you haven't yet got a clue about what the *future* holds.

Confusion is for most people a symptom of being *on* the bridge. 'Con' means 'with' and fusion means 'together' in Latin; that is, 'together with'. Therefore, con-fusion is the old reality happening *together* with the new reality.

Looked at this way, confusion is a significant element of change. 'A' is the old reality, 'C' is the new reality, and 'B' (the transition from A to C) is confusion. I'm not saying that confusion necessarily feels good. Moving from the old reality into our right livelihood doesn't necessarily happen while we are doing cartwheels and whistling 'Dixie'.

So let's not forget about 'worry' as part of the transition package. It's often part of the same stew as confusion. Worry is actually an uncompleted cycle. For example, we are worried because our three-month-old puppy has found his way out of our fenced yard and is gone. We do all of the obvious things to find him, all the while feeling worried. Then a neighbour brings him home: end of worry – the cycle completed. As life is an endless series of uncompleted cycles, there's considerable wisdom in the phrase, 'Don't worry, be happy.'

Transition includes realistic self-appraisal and accepting where you are *now*, as discussed in the previous chapter. It also requires planning.

Planning

Planning can be a critical part of minimising the confusion of transition. If you have three minutes in the day, use one to plan the other two.

Getting in the habit of effective planning produces terrific rewards; it is a *must*. It supports us in valuing and using our time wisely. Planning is an example of form which enhances our direction and purpose.

Naturally, the only way to get anywhere else is to leave where you are now. Sound simple? Of course it is! Yet you'd be surprised at how many people commit to moving to the next step without being sufficiently clear about where they are now. Often we are propelled to take the next step because we are experiencing various forms of discomfort with our present situation and we don't like the feeling.

Take time to inventory your present situation, because if you don't you *will* move to the next place and you *will* take your old baggage with you. In other words, get clear on your *motivation* for wanting to develop your right livelihood. How much of it has to do with your real passion and how much of it is that you just don't want to be where you are now – or that you don't want to feel all of your feelings? The process of moving forward usually involves a bit of each.

With an effective inventory you can determine whether you want to step into your right livelihood on a part-time basis, or whether you want to quit your job and begin your new livelihood full-time.

Making an inventory may even help you fine-tune the job you have now. It may lead you to ask the boss for less and/or different hours, more money or a different position. Quite often employers are willing to make changes with regard to certain valued employees rather than lose them. I've seen it happen. However, often when people are ready to quit their job they haven't given any thought to going to their boss and saying, 'Hey, this isn't working.' When they do, they often find the boss quite receptive to what they have to say. They negotiate with the boss, and this results in them staying on in their position in a way that works for everyone.

Designing and Developing the Career you Want

For example, Craig and Vanessa were newly married and enjoying a DINK (Double Income, No Kids) lifestyle. Craig worked for a small computer software company and was highly regarded professionally and well-liked by his colleagues. However, soon after their wedding Craig's job stress began to increase, and subsequently affected his relationship with Vanessa.

It got to the point where Craig was planning to leave his job because he was fast approaching burnout. Over dinner one evening, Vanessa proposed a rather obvious and simple suggestion. She said to Craig, 'Why don't you talk to Doug [Craig's boss] and see if you can work something out with him?' The next day Craig had a chat with Doug and told him about the situation. Doug didn't want to lose him so they negotiated that Craig would work part-time. As a consequence, the couple's income decreased temporarily (although Craig was able to pick up some independent consulting work); however, the harmony at home was infinitely greater.

I do not advocate 'throwing out the baby with the bath water'. See what can work best for you after you have completed your inventory.

Functional change

Functional change, as I describe it, is a *balance* of awareness and action. One of the symptoms associated with having lots of awarenesses can be inertia. An overwhelming number of possibilities and choices – along with the extraordinary insights we might have – keep us stuck.

Ask yourself if you are using your insights and awarenesses as additional ammunition to beat yourself up with. Are you saying to yourself, 'Not only is this area of my life not working, I know exactly *why* it is not working'? Does the fact remain that the particular area of your life is still not working? Awareness by itself does not produce change.

Are you paralysed when it comes to action-taking, too? Are you so immersed in your daily work, as dissatisfying as it is, that you are not acting to change it? Are you stuck in a rut? If you are saying you are *too* busy to take time for yourself then you are just *too* busy, full stop. If you're really unhappy, you can't afford *not* to take some time for honest evaluation of things and research into what is causing your discontent.

The components of functional change, as I've said, include planning, making an orderly transition, ensuring you have adequate financial reserves and seeing things with clarity. Clarity is a result of realistic self-appraisal (see Chapter 1); even though you may not be clear on *where* you want to go, you certainly want to be clear on where you are *now*. Often our emotions tell us something isn't working when, in fact, it is; we just need to see it clearly.

There is a difference between prioritising our tasks to get to the next step, jolly and jaunty, and *running* to the next step because our emotions are propelling us. Once again, ask yourself your *motivation* for developing your right livelihood.

How important is your career/job to you really?

Most people suffer about career and money not because they are unimportant, but because they are not really important *enough* to them. They treat money and career as things they do and things that simply happen.

How much time have you invested in researching money and career matters? When was the last time you went to the library, business centre or local bookshop and took home books or tapes on career development and/or the psychology of money?

If you have not spent time doing these things, remember that developing your right livelihood is not about getting another job in order to keep on simply surviving. You are crafting your right livelihood so that it allows you to express all that you are, highlighting your creativity and sparking your passion. It's about finding daily life work that is in alignment with your values and what is in your heart.

Are you entangled in your 'real' job?

Entanglement is defined as 'that from which escape is difficult'. Are you entangled in your 'real' job?

Are you in a situation similar to that of a dog chasing its tail? Do you know it is time to change your present job and do something different, yet you are staying put because there are bills to be paid, or you're afraid there is nothing else available for you 'out there'? Are you staying put because it is familiar to you and, as such, comfortable? Or are you sticking to your 'real' job simply because you have developed close friendships with people you work with?

If you answered 'yes' to any of these questions, you may be entangled.

Departmental thinking

One of the great obstacles to developing your right livelihood is departmental thinking. Departmental thinking is living life in little boxes: for example, thinking in terms of your 'work life', 'financial life', 'home life', 'social life', 'creative life' or 'love life'. We know these areas are related to each other; however, often we live our daily lives as if they were not. We tend to say things such as, 'I am going off to work', 'I am going to spend time with my family', 'I am going to work out', 'I am going on a holiday to the Great Barrier Reef'. Then, with each of these statements, society tends to collude in this seemingly universal understanding that life is split up, with declarations such as, 'You're going to work? Ah, too bad!' or 'You're going on holiday? That's great!'

Developing our right livelihood helps to heal the separations, so that the gulf between work and play shrinks. George Hallus, former coach of the champion Chicago Bears American football team, once said, 'It's not work unless you'd rather be doing something else.' Do you want to be doing something else?

As you develop your right livelihood you need to look at your judgements about your actions in life. Judgements create separation, especially the judgements that say things such as, 'This is the material world', 'This is the spiritual world', and so on. Einstein once said, 'There's no such thing as spirit and matter. There's only spirit in denser form.' As you create your right livelihood you can reframe many limiting concepts and judgements. You can begin to bring your business to your consciousness and your consciousness to your business.

Bringing business to consciousness

Bringing business to consciousness gives you an opportunity to bring together the different parts of your life and let go of the judgements you have formed around them.

I believe that each of us has a dance to dance, a play to act and a song to sing, and that each of these things is unique to each of us. It is our own personal and intimate gift to ourselves and to the world. What *we are* is the universe's gift to us, what *we become* is our gift to the universe. As we become more of who we really are, not just our conditioning, the separations in life become less obvious. This is bringing business to consciousness.

Bringing consciousness to business

Today, businesses, ranging from small companies to multinationals, are becoming more sensitive and responsive to the environment, and to the needs of their employees, including providing benefits such as parental leave, flexible working schedules, environmental programs and profit-sharing programs.

Of course, this transition doesn't happen without a certain amount of struggle and confusion. The question is: is *your* business a co-operative community citizen? Or do you *work for* a business that is a co-operative community citizen? Is it/are you responsive to the needs of planet earth and its people?

Look at what you can do to become more mindful of your responsibilities in this area. Begin a recycling program, for example. Initiate car pooling. Tailor work schedules for your employees. What can *you* do to bring consciousness to business?

Habit building

When you talk about staying with what is familiar, paying the bills, surviving, and the like, are you simply staying put because it is a habit? A lot that happens in our work world is simply habit. According to some research, it can take from twenty-one to twenty-eight days to build a habit. Conversely, it can take from twenty-one to twenty-eight days to break a habit.

What do *you* do that is habit? When was the last time you took a different route to work? When was the last time you took a different mode of transportation to work? When was the last time you moved your desk around at work?

As an experiment do something different at work for the next twenty-eight days. For example, have lunch at a different time, write with a different coloured pen, bring flowers into your office. Doing this may help get you out of the feeling of being stuck you are experiencing in your present position.

You could also make an inventory of your work-related habits. Once you have done this, have a look at the habits that are still producing results. What habits can be changed to serve you better during this time of transition towards your right livelihood? Making small non-threatening changes opens the way to making bigger ones.

Over time we can consciously build habits. We can become aware of what habits we have and what habits we want: work, planning and prioritising habits. A habit can be mindless or it can be mindful.

Do an inventory of your life to find out which of your habits are mindless and which are mindful.

Shock and repetition

Research has shown that humans learn in only one of two ways: shock or repetition. For years I have challenged behavioural scientists, psychologists, sociologists and anthropologists to find a third way. In the final analysis they cannot. Shock and repetition work this way: we burn our fingers on the stove and typically we don't do it over and over again. Occasionally we *do* do it again, which, invariably, is a rude reminder of what we have learned.

In my personal coaching work I use affirmations. These are often boring; yet through repetition they produce results. Writing an affirmation seventy times a day for seven days gives the subconscious a different message from the one it is already receiving.

How much of your daily work life is simply a result of habits and patterns? (A pattern is 'unconscious, repetitive behaviour'.) The first step you need to take is to make the behaviour *conscious*. The second step is to 'choose out'. This means that every time you become aware you are engaging in that particular behaviour – STOP! By repeating this process over and over, the pattern can cease to exist. Remember though, you want to inventory those habits and patterns that still serve you well, and are productive for change.

In a 'real' job there is always the chance of getting fired. This may be due to downsizing, bankruptcy, relocation, technology, personality stuff, company politics and a host of other reasons. This takes away the security and certainty of having a 'real' job, and when it happens is often a shock. The intensity of the shock is usually in direct proportion to how much denial the person is in. It's the difference between the shock of stubbing your toe on a chair leg and crashing your car into a pole.

How many times do you need to get fired or relocated to know that 'real' jobs have certain limitations and don't offer total security?

The eight Ps in creating our passionate right livelihood

This is a handy, dandy way to help you see your relationship to your life work with more clarity.

Saint Augustine said, 'The reward of patience is patience.' Are you in a big hurry to develop your right livelihood because you are uncomfortable with your present situation? Are you unhappy with your life now because of other things that are not related to work? Perhaps your home life is strained. Maybe you are dealing with problems associated with your physical body.

It's easy to *say* 'be patient' to yourself, and not so easy to *be* patient if you don't consider yourself to be a patient person. To embrace your present situation fully is to accept your feelings and emotions while you are crossing the bridge one step at a time. You can cultivate *patience* by striving to accept things as they are, rather than run from where you are because you are trying to escape those feelings.

If you are spending most of your life dealing with career and money issues, then make them a top *priority*. The trick is not necessarily to prioritise your *schedule*, it's rather to schedule your *priorities*. Where you are going is more important than getting there quickly. Goethe said, 'Things which matter most must never be at the mercy of things which matter least.'

By being patient with ourselves and prioritising work, life and money, we can begin to develop the next step – *perseverance*, or the art of 'keeping on keeping on'. Perseverance is sometimes affected by the capricious nature of everyday life and we can make life more palatable when we find the *pleasure* in developing the career of our dreams.

While you are doing the left-brain work of *planning* (as discussed earlier) and prioritising, you can also balance it with the right-brain activity of taking time daily to close your eyes and let your body feel exactly what it's like to be living and enjoying pursuing your right livelihood. We can often persevere more effectively if we visualise, imagine and write about what our dream would look like. We persevere until we can virtually taste it, smell it, hear it, see it and touch it.

The next P is *profit*, which I define as anything produced for gain. The most obvious connotation of the term is financial return, yet it is certainly not limited to this. I look at profit as a way of measuring my emotional, spiritual return on my contribution to the people in my life.

Protection is the effective management of financial resources. You can avoid putting yourself in a position of scarcity while you are developing your right livelihood. When you are developing your right livelihood you are merely witnessing the full and free expression of your creative energy as it relates to taking your passion to the marketplace. Make sure you have enough to live on before embarking on this adventure.

Also, don't let *pride* stand in the way. It has been said that 'Pride goeth before a fall.' Are you willing to do whatever it takes, *no matter what*, or will pride step in the way? I am not talking about pride in having, doing and being something; I am talking about the *false* pride that keeps us from being assertive, and honestly asking ourselves and others, clearly and simply, for what we want with no attachment to the results. It's 'graduate work' – knowing that you are always responsible for your actions. You are not always responsible for the results.

Chapter 3
The People Business

*'I've never seen a business fail in my life.
Businesses don't fail. People do.'* – Stefan Smith

Millionaire James Tollison says, 'Dealing with, getting along with, and associating with other people is the business we are *all* in.' Effective, functional and therefore healthy relationships with our colleagues and associates can bring us valuable emotional satisfaction. Conversely, our work relationships can cause us some of our biggest headaches.

If you are currently employed, about to be unemployed, already unemployed, contemplating starting a new business, about to go into someone else's business, or already engaged in a new business, your success is directly related to how you understand yourself in relationship to others and how you understand others in relationship to yourself.

Other people have an effect on our energy. We need to accumulate energy to work to get our job done while having to put up with individuals we work with. It's unfortunate that many people invest their energy in putting up with, dealing with, getting along with and working with others who are *no* fun to play with.

More often than not, at work we duplicate our place in our family. The extent and nature of our unresolved family issues will reflect the extent to which we find ourselves challenged by certain people's behaviours at work. These people unconsciously trigger unresolved family patterns. Some classic symptoms of family dysfunction that we may find ourselves playing out at work could include abuse, abandonment, neglect and enmeshment.

Abuse

There are many forms of abuse. The ones you have probably heard about most often are physical and sexual abuse. There is also mental, emotional and psychic abuse.

We typically think of abuse as being intense and dramatic. However, some forms of abuse can be very subtle, yet have significant impact on the victim. Bosses and co-workers can be abusive, and so can certain work environments, in aspects ranging from the quality of air in the office to the acoustics of the workplace.

Abandonment

Abandonment can affect people because of what happened to them in the first six or so years of life when their personalities were in the process of being formed. What occurred may be as simple as feeling abandoned because Dad went off to work each morning. Later, issues of abandonment may come up in the workplace.

An example of abandonment in the office would be being given a task to do without being given instructions and appropriate support, and guidance on how to perform it. We are then abandoned to the task. Left to our own devices, a range of emotions is triggered, and this may ultimately result in the job not getting done efficiently and our ensuing frustration. It may also trigger thoughts such as, 'I should know how to do this', leading to feelings of inadequacy.

Neglect

Being neglected means our needs aren't being taken care of. There are many ways to be 'neglected' in the office, and they include, yet are not limited to, the physical ones. For example, you are not permitted sufficient lunch breaks or tea breaks, there is no toilet paper, there are no windows, the airconditioning is faulty, or the office is dirty. Lack of communication from superiors, or acknowledgement of what you have done, is also a form of neglect.

Enmeshment

Enmeshment occurs when healthy, and therefore clearly-defined, boundaries have not been established between people. For example, when you were young what happened when Dad lost his temper? Did he express anger *at* you *for* something you *did*? In a truly functional and healthy family Dad would have expressed his anger and that would usually have been OK. It would have been clear to everyone else that it was *Dad's* anger, it belonged to him, he 'owned' it, and it had nothing to do with you. What you did triggered Dad's anger – it didn't cause his anger.

However, anger may have been expressed when we did or didn't do something the way our parents wanted us to. As a result most of us have never come to understand our boundaries or emotions.

Because we tend to duplicate our family relationships at work, we can become aware of our experiences and the dynamics involved, and use this for personal healing. We can observe ourselves and the roles we play. We can monitor our responses to particular individuals and situations, and take note of our repetitive behaviour. We can also study and become aware of others' responses to our behaviours. If we run our own business we can learn a lot from our clients, employees and associates.

Attracting the ideal customer, client, patient, audience

Creating your right livelihood (in the way your heart truly desires) involves hanging out with clients and customers who get the job done and are *fun to play with*. If this sounds like a tall order, then remember, you *do* create your own reality. There are no exceptions to this. If you think there are, then you may like to do a quick inventory.

- **Ask yourself the following questions:**
- What do I want?
- Why do I want it?
- Why *don't* I want it?
- What does my past tell me about having this?
- What do my fears say?
- What do I really desire?
  What do I honestly expect?

Then what?

Visualisation

Often the people I work with exclaim, 'Are you saying if we have a retail shop, we can decide what kind of customer comes in off the street? You're kidding!' No, I'm not! Each and every one of us has the potential and the power to have it the way we want it using visualisation.

I've seen retailers get clear and specific about the type of customer they want and, to their astonishment, notice a change within thirty days, when a different kind of customer walks in. A couple I worked with recently found, after using the techniques discussed in this book, that the number of browsers who came into their store dropped. On the other hand, the average individual sales volume increased. By getting clear and focused, and employing visualisation techniques, they were able to attract people who browsed less, bought more, and were fun to play with.

A chiropractor I know juggled 185 patient visits a week. As a result he was fast approaching burnout and his home life was suffering. He loved what he did, yet was overworked because he thought he had to keep the number of his patients' visits high to support his practice and therefore his family. When he did an inventory and practised visualisation techniques, he was able to get clear and focused on the type of patient he really wanted to work with. Subsequently he increased his fees, and was able to attract clients who took more personal responsibility for their health, didn't whinge about fees and were more fun to play with. This left him with more time and energy for his family and leisure pursuits.

Working with others can provide the best training ground for developing effective, functional and joyous relationships. You may say, 'I don't have any choice about who I work with, I'm an employee.' That's true; yet you can always choose how you respond to others, react to things and invite others to be with you. You can take responsibility and create the work relationships you want.

In one of the 'real' jobs I had, I worked with a hostile secretary who had been with the company 'forever'. She always seemed annoyed with me. She was always huffy and short in her responses to me. Part of me was quite intimidated by her. She was well up on corporate politics and over the years had developed strong relationships with my superiors. I couldn't simply give her her walking papers without dealing with lots of fallout.

I used a number of different tactics, none of which worked, and after a while I actually started to dread going to work. I phoned a wise friend of mine, described my predicament, and asked for some feedback. His message was simple, yet brilliant. Initially, he said, 'Have you done any visualisation?' At first I didn't know what he meant. 'Visualisation?' He then went on to clarify what he had said. 'Aren't you the one who is always running around saying there is one consciousness and we are all one? Is that just more of this New Age prattle?'

The next morning before I left the house I took a minute to visualise my secretary the way I would have liked her to be, as I wanted myself to be with her and how I wanted us to be together. I noticed nothing for four days, then on the fifth day I walked into the office and was astounded to find her attitude transformed. Over time we began to work well together, and actually enjoy each other's company.

Taking time to visualise how we would like a relationship to be, while being patient and accepting of the situation, is a handy trick to help transform those difficult relationships at work. First, begin by accepting the situation exactly as it is without judgment, blame or criticism; second, visualise the situation as you would like it to be. Over time you will notice a shift. This can work with *any* relationship, whether it be with your boss, supervisor or co-worker.

As a cautionary note, be keenly aware of the difference between expectation and healthy anticipation. Expectation can often be a set-up for disappointment. Healthy anticipation, on the other hand, doesn't have an attachment to results. Expectation is a destination, while healthy anticipation is a journey.

Many of the 168 hours in our week are invested in our life work. Therefore, we give ourselves a powerful gift if we can cultivate work relationships that support, nourish and enliven us.

Task, relationship and harmony

Most people fit into one of two broad categories when it comes to them establishing their own business – they are *task* people or *relationship* people.

If you are task orientated you will create your business based more on the functions of the work you do. If you are relationship orientated, then relationships are the focus of your business. This may mean you are likely to go into business with a friend or acquaintance. In both of these categories you can be fast or slow: that is, perform tasks quickly or slowly, or form relationships quickly or slowly. You may also be a combination of these, and the combination may change at different times.

Generally speaking, creating your right livelihood in partnership is not recommended unless you have established trust with the other person or persons, and an honest, safe and open way of communicating with them. This will allow you to discuss where and how you are, and are not, aligned with one another. If you're not aligned, the business or project may start to unravel.

Being in alignment

Over the years I have been using a powerful process for people who want to start a project together to find out whether they are aligned:

- Each person involved in the project defines their purpose within the project.
- Each person then compares their individual purpose with everyone else in the group.

- Each individual shares their vision of the purpose of the project.
- Each person compares their vision of the group purpose with that of the others in the group.

This simple technique can be performed in the boardroom of a multinational company, with a partner in a small business or with other associates.

Obviously, conflict is going to arise in areas where people are out of alignment with each other. This may not be apparent at first. In the beginning, whether it be a business relationship or a relationship with a co-worker, there is generally an initial enthusiasm that will produce creative rewards and results. After the honeymoon, however, conflict may arise.

The elements of successful business

There are resources available to assist you in establishing your right livelihood and dealing effectively with others. Some of the most important of these are people. For example, aside from books, there are seminars, counsellors and therapists, or you may know of someone who has been through an experience similar to yours and learned from it.

In dealing with others, the subconscious has a *huge* investment in keeping us to what is familiar, because of the risks involved in branching out. That is, people are often dunked when they are on the crest of success. If we are approaching success or have been enjoying success for a while, we may find some way to flush it down the loo. I've seen this happen with lots of people who are developing their right livelihood. It doesn't matter what they are doing, there can be the prospect of sabotage lurking, that is, they may crash their car, lose some money, break up with a partner or become ill. One of the elements of success is to be able to recognise when we are beginning to get away from the basics that produced the success to begin with.

Businesses never fail

I have never seen a business fail in my life. Businesses don't 'fail', people do. When we create our right livelihood as a business, it's important to know *what we don't know*. A great idea, passion, the right timing, are simply not enough. If we have never had a business, or have had a business that has 'failed', then support from others is vital.

Please note that I don't use 'failure' in the traditional sense, because I believe there is no such thing as failure if you learn from it. When Thomas Edison invented the light bulb, he trialed over 900 different configurations of gases, filaments, etc., before ... Bingo!, he 'saw the light'. Edison apparently didn't consider the previous 900 experiments failures because he learned from each of them. A champion American football player was once asked during an interview, 'How does it feel to hold the world's record for the most completed passes?' He replied, 'It feels pretty good – and what you guys don't realise is, I also hold the world's record for the most uncompleted passes!'

There is an abundance of information available to help guide and support you in creating your right livelihood as a successful business. Napoleon Hill, in his international bestselling book *Think And Grow Rich*, researched the traits, characteristics, habits and attitudes of successful people, and was able to extract a handful of basic principles. Although it was written some time ago, it remains a classic.

If you know a person who has, or has had, a successful business, you may want to ask them for a few pointers. Successful people are often available and enjoy helping others. They usually 'remember when' themselves. If you don't ask for advice, help and support you have a 100 per cent chance of not getting any. If you do ask, you cut the chance down to 50 per cent.

We want to take action, especially if there is fear, anxiety, or resistance triggered. These feelings usually tell us we are on the right path and give us an opportunity to *fear forward*.

Utilise your available resources, know what you don't know, and be humble. My definition of the word humility is 'teachability'. Are you willing to be coached when you take the next step towards creating your right livelihood?

It's important, however, to remember not to let anyone talk you out of your dreams. I think this reference to starting a business is a little narrow in the context of the book. Opinions are like noses: there are no two alike, so don't let anyone 'rain on your parade'.

Professional advice

I can't emphasise enough the value of professional advice. When you are creating your right livelihood as a business, rely on the help of top professionals to ensure its success. There are professionals in the areas of marketing, management, finance and operations you could talk to, who have probably forgotten more than others will ever know about these systems. (It's a bonus if they also happen to love what they do.) Once again, typically the more successful an individual is in their chosen area, the more generous they are with their time and experience.

What if you *really* are not a people person? You love to paint, write, make music, and know in your heart you 'march to a different drummer', and that this march doesn't particularly involve other people. I have worked with artistic and creative people, ranging from computer operators to sculptors, who are completely happy and fulfilled living the beauty of their dreams alone. Again, the key is to become teachable. Know your limitations. Hire a business manager etc., to represent you. Allow others to handle your business affairs. Having your business systems in order will free up your time and allow you to do what you really love, as opposed to getting bogged down and enmeshed in daily administration and operations.

Competition

When you bring consciousness to business there is no such thing as competition. Instead, there is an attitude that abundance exists; this can inspire you to new creative heights so that you can build and design a better business. This is a more expansive way to look at 'competition' (I thought competition didn't exist when you bring consciousness to business?).

I know a man in New Zealand who owns a wonderful shop full of books, crystals, tapes, and an array of other products designed to nurture and delight the child within. When a similar shop opened across the street, he saw it as taking business away from him. I told him, 'Your place is quite different. *You* are different. There's more than enough for everyone. While it was a tough one for him, he did get his head around the concept. As a result he wound up moving to a better location and expanding the size of his shop.

Competition is something people often look at when they are creating their right livelihood. For example, if you want to open a shop selling recycled goods, you will ask yourself, 'Is there anyone else in town who has this kind of shop?' If this is a concern, open up *your* shop and give it a different flair, a different focus, a different attitude – and remember you are *always* in the *people business*. That alone will usually make you stand out from the crowd.

Recently, I went into a shop to pick up a particular greeting card from a line that the shop carried. I couldn't find the card so I asked the shopkeeper about it, and they quickly and curtly responded, 'No, we don't have it.' Cool. I went down the street to another shop with the same line of greeting cards. Again, I didn't see the card so I asked the shopkeeper. She said: 'No, but hang on a minute, I'll call the rep. If it's in that line, we'll be able to get it for you. How many do you want? When do you want them? Do you want to pick them up here? Or do you want me to send them out to you?' She went the extra mile with a smile and from then on had a regular customer – me!

I frequent businesses because of their attitude; I go to places where I am welcomed and there is an expression of gratitude for my custom.

The three virtues in communication

Working with others is a grand and glorious opportunity to take our relationship skills to a higher level. This includes establishing healthy boundaries and expressing ourselves honestly with *courage, self-discipline* and *gracefulness* – the three virtues of communication.

Most of us would see one of these three virtues as a major challenge.

Courage

If courage is our challenge we would tend to suppress our feelings rather than express them. Our self-talk is, 'I'll say it later', or 'It doesn't really matter'. Or somehow we rationalise our desire to express what is on our mind by saying, 'I'll just accept it the way it is', when in actual fact it may be more appropriate (although uncomfortable) to speak out about what is really going on inside us.

Self-discipline

If self-discipline is our challenge we may blurt out our frustrations or concerns in a way that is inappropriate, being, for example, hurtful or inflammatory. Mastering self-discipline involves taking a moment, getting in touch with yourself, and mentally 'hearing' what your response might sound like. You would then carefully choose the right words.

Gracefulness

If gracefulness is our challenge, then we find it difficult to say what we mean clearly in a way that embraces the other person.

One of your co-workers – let's call her Fran – may be an incessant talker. Fran likes to come and sit on top of your desk – even though the chair next to the desk is empty – while you are working. You are in the middle of a critical project. Fran has no concept of boundaries and launches into one of her monologues of meaningless drivel while sitting on your desk. How do you react?

If your challenge is *courage* you would suppress your feelings and pray every day that Fran would get the sack. If your challenge is self-discipline you might turn to Fran and say, 'You really bug me. Get out of my face.' If your challenge is gracefulness you may say, 'Fran, umm, err, uhh ..., Fran would you sit in the chair?' Fran, of course, doesn't get it because you are not asking her *not* to sit on the desk. However, if you have mastered the three virtues of communication you may sound like this: 'Fran, I'm getting this project organised and I'd appreciate it if you sat in the chair when you came over. Does that work for you?' Or you might say, 'I'm busy right now. I have a tight deadline to meet. Would you mind if we chatted another time?'

Conflict resolution

Author, anthropologist and researcher Angeles Arrien defines conflict as 'a situation of change and/or a situation that provides growth'. Conflict is a dynamic most of us haven't learned to handle well, even though it comes as part and parcel of every relationship. In her research into cross-cultural anthropology, Arrien found two primary causes of conflict or misunderstanding in most countries:

- Not saying what we mean.
- Not doing what we say.

Mastering these two behaviours can be the most effective ways to resolve workplace conflict.

Saying what we mean, even though we are doing it with self-discipline, courage and gracefulness, may evoke an uncomfortable reaction at times. Are you willing to express appropriately *all* of who you are with boldness?

How many times have you associated with people who say they will do something and rarely do it? Their words don't seem to be connected to any real intention. We all know people like this. Perhaps we have been, or are, one of them. Because we want to be liked and accepted, we haven't yet been able to have the freedom that comes from saying the word 'no'. Sometimes saying 'no' to others can be an empowering way of saying 'yes' to ourselves. Simple? Yes. Easy? Not necessarily.

We know that saying 'no' will at times cause conflict. Remember the story of the bus driver in the first chapter?

There was an immediate and obvious potential for conflict. My choice was to minimise it and still get what I wanted. I chose to deal with the conflict by giving the bus driver three choices: call the police, call his superintendent or accept that I was going to ride the bus. It was resolved quickly and simply because I had made up my mind to deal with any one of his choices. I felt he was clearly out of line, and no matter what, I was riding that bus.

Conflict resolution involves taking responsibility for how you feel, how you think and how you express the way you are feeling. For example, instead of pointing the finger and saying, 'You said ...', point the finger at yourself and say, 'I heard you say ...'. It's important to word it in a way that doesn't threaten the other person, and doesn't imply that you are judging, blaming or criticising them. This creates the safety in which you can communicate effectively and creates a win/win situation.

There are exceptions to this, of course. Say, for example, I ran over your foot with my bicycle. It's appropriate for you to say, 'Stefan, you really hurt me when you ran over my foot with your bicycle.' However, if you're still going on about it the following week, then it's time for you to take responsibility. I am no longer hurting you – you're now hurting yourself. Taking responsibility is discussed in more detail below.

Listening is also extremely important when it comes to conflict resolution. Angeles Arrien writes, 'Most conflict arises when people feel unheard and unseen.' She suggests these six steps to conflict resolution:

1. Identify the problem.
2. Brainstorm at least ten possible solutions to the problem.
3. Select the three most workable ones from the list.
4. Negotiate with others to reach a consensus on the single most workable solution.

5. Create and implement a plan to carry out the decision.
6. Set up a time frame in which to review how the solution is working and how it may need to be refined.

Wars are fought, divorces happen, partnerships break up, families fight, road rage occurs, people kill, companies become bankrupt, all because many people haven't yet managed the art and science of conflict resolution. I've heard it said that 'Discussion is an exchange of knowledge; argument an exchange of emotion'.

Taking responsibility

When you meet a predicament or confrontation, it's helpful to keep this axiom in mind: 'I am only responsible for my actions – *never* their results.' Let me qualify this. Any reasonable, sensible and sensitive individual knows if they say certain things and take certain actions, it is going to illicit a predictable reaction or response in another person. We *don't* say and do things we know will deliberately hurt, harm or otherwise upset others. When we recognise and practise this, we know we can never be responsible for the reactions of others. We have really done our best.

For example, one summer I was doing a sales training for a middle-management sales team. We left early one Friday afternoon and, to illustrate this axiom, I got in the elevator on the top floor of a twelve-storey building and stood with my back against the front wall across from the control panel. (People usually have their back towards the back wall of the elevator.) When people got in I was careful not to make eye contact with anyone or make faces.

When the elevator reached the lobby and the doors opened, one man looked at me, shook his head in disgust and exited the elevator posthaste. Another woman shook her head in disdain. There were a couple of people who remained stony-faced as they exited. There was one person who smiled. Then there was this couple who I had never seen before. When we reached the lobby, without saying a word one gently grabbed my right elbow, the other my left, and we walked out into the lobby and onto the sidewalk, giggling all the while. Then they disappeared and I never saw them again.

Later, I asked the trainees how many actions I had taken and everyone was in agreement: 'One.' Then I asked how many reactions there were. We counted at least four.

Boundaries

Healthy boundaries are born of a clear sense of self. They also involve allowing and accepting others' behaviours with the understanding that *we are not our behaviours*. For example, if a four year old takes a box of crayons and scribbles all over the dining room wall, we let them know that that's not allowed. We continue to love them and know they are not their behaviours. The trick is doing this with adults!

If you have a functional sense of self you will be accepting of others, and at the same time let them know there are certain behaviours you won't allow. Communicating your boundaries with courage, self-discipline and gracefulness contributes to a more harmonious situation in the workplace, and, on a larger scale, to peace in the world.

Chapter 4
It's Never About the Money

*'Hoping to extinguish the drive for riches with
money is like pouring butter fat on a fire, attempting
to extinguish it.'* – Hindu expression

It's *never* about the money! It's about your *attitude* to money. Have you been using money as a way of keeping yourself from expressing all that you are? Have you been using money to keep you stuck in what is familiar to you? Have you been using money to create the illusion of safety? Have you been using money as a way of maintaining relationships with others that no longer serve you? Have you been using money as a way of intimidating yourself? Have you been using money to feed your anxiety? Worry? Depression? Fear? Feelings of scarcity, lack and awareness of limitation? If you have, rejoice knowing that's no longer necessary. You *can* use money to nourish your soul, enliven your spirits and express your joy.

Money often represents freedom and security. Yet, if you are looking to money to provide you with real security, certainty and freedom, then you're barking up the wrong tree.

Money can be a convenient place to put our fears

Over 25 per cent of the people I have worked with over the years have had multi-million dollar portfolios. They came to me because they weren't finding balance and harmony in *all* areas of their life.

I remember the newspaper story of one man found living as a derelict in his own home. It was littered with trash and falling apart. The garden was overgrown and was a junk lover's delight. No one would have guessed that this man was worth over two million dollars! This is the nature of 'poverty consciousness', which is a state of mind that *always* feels poor.

Channel PBS (Public Broadcasting System) in the United States featured an interesting program on lottery winners. Ten families, who had each won a multi-million dollar lottery, were interviewed. (In the United States, winners are paid annual payments, after tax is taken out, over a twenty-year period.) They found after interviewing these families that they were invariably in worse shape financially after twenty years than before they had won the lottery. None of the winners had invested wisely, managed their money effectively or planned for the future. Instead, they became overnight mega-consumers, and wound up with very little to show for their windfalls. Fear is what motivates some multimillionaires I have worked with. Even after they have made their money, the fear is still present, only now their fear is of losing the money.

One of the easiest and most functional ways to attract money to yourself is to find *inner* freedom and security. Most of us see things in reverse. We think we will have freedom and security *when* we win the lottery, discover gold on our property, inherit a fortune, invent the hula hoop or find an oil well. It's all about 'when I'. Yet it's not about *when*, it's about *now*.

How much of your present happiness are you sacrificing for some future condition? Begin *now* to accept gratefully your financial life exactly as it is. It is through acceptance of your present situation that change can occur. Begin at the beginning.

Money as an abstraction

The more abstract something is, the more powerful it is. Common abstractions include love, beauty, truth and nature. Money is in the same category as these. Mastering money can provide us with an incredible opportunity to end our 'separations'; that is, the 'material' world is no longer separated from the so-called 'spiritual' world. They are one and the same.

People often ask me, 'Where's the spiritual world?' I respond, 'Where *isn't* it?' As Einstein said, 'There's no such thing as spirit and matter, there's only spirit in denser form.'

Steam is abstract. We can see it; we can't hold it. Yet, in a different form, steam becomes water, and then ice. It's the same substance in three different forms. Money, too, comes in many different shapes. It is an energy that wears many costumes.

Money as an energy

Everything is a form of energy. As with the water analogy above, money is energy in different forms. Money in modern society symbolises energy exchanges. We use money to pay for goods and services. It is passed back and forward, around and around, inside out, upside down.

Nothing is ever created or destroyed. It simply changes form. As a form of energy, money can be changed into other forms. There are the material forms such as what we can see and touch, and there are other forms, such as investment. Money as an energy can be used to create more money. It's a continual flow.

I have often seen people increase their income when they embark on creating their right livelihood. One of the reasons for this is their increased expression of creative and emotional energy. This in turn attracts more energy in the form of money. It's not unusual to see people double their income when they get established in their right livelihood.

Tithing as one way of attracting money

If you really want to attract money to yourself, consider tithing. In ancient times a tithe was a tax. It involved paying one-tenth of what you had, that is, every tenth pig or 10 per cent of a crop. If ten householders lived near each other, tithing (or taking tithe) also implied taking responsibility for each other's peaceable behaviour. Tithing in contemporary communities has a similar, yet different; connotation.

Tithing, as we use the term now, is simply the act of giving away 10 per cent of all money that we receive as profit. We can give the money to a charitable organisation, or to an author, a musician, a friend or a teacher: that is, to an individual or organisation from whom or which we get our 'spiritual food'. The money should be given consciously, and with gratitude and love. A tithe is a personal way to give back to the universe.

With tithing you can balance what you receive by giving freely. It's a way of tapping into the limitless abundance of the universe. Tithing also shows us that working harder does not necessarily bring in more money – abundance is dependent on our beliefs, not necessarily on a flurry of activities.

It's Never About the Money

An early 'tithing teacher' gave me $50 because she considered me to be a source of 'spiritual food'. She suggested I open a tithing account at the bank and make this money my first deposit. I tithed 10 per cent of it to someone I considered to be a source of spiritual food and opened the account with $45. Within six weeks the account grew to $600. I was tithing 10 per cent of everything that came to me into this account. When I finally closed the account, I gave all the money in it to twelve different people whom I considered to be sources of 'spiritual food' – a teacher, a number of supportive friends, a couple of authors, my sisters and a mentor. The entire experience allowed me to see myself in a new light and to accept my rightful abundance.

It's difficult to believe we can ease a financial jam by spending money. Yet some kind of magic happens when we open ourselves up to, and develop a trust in, the universal flow. Tithing gives us an opportunity to move through old patterns that tell us 'There's never enough'.

If you feel broke, spend some money frivolously. You may buy an ice-cream for a kid, donate $5 to a homeless person, give $20 to a busker. By doing so you are affirming that 'I have enough'. The truth is, if you have food, shelter, clothing, and a dollar in your pocket, then you have *more* than enough. If you don't feel that way, then there's work to do. The reality of your financial life is that you *do* have enough. Sometimes our mind can agree yet fear immobilises us from taking action. The trick is to feel the fear of not having enough and give 10 per cent of it away anyway.

In a workshop in New Zealand I asked the participants, 'How many people in here have more than enough money?' No-one raised their hand. I then asked, 'How many do not have food, shelter or clothing?' Nobody raised their hand. My final question was, 'How many have at least five cents in their pocket?' Everybody raised their hand. I then said, 'Everybody here has more than enough.' If we don't know we have more than enough right now, then we can win lotto, discover gold, inherit or make a fortune, and still feel like it's not enough.

Whatever we give away is returned to us tenfold. When I asked one of my prosperity teachers, 'Can I give *more* than 10 per cent?', she replied, 'How much do you want to get back?'

Of course, we want to balance our tithing with effective money management. Certainly, starting with 10 per cent for a while can be a grand experiment. Give it a whirl. You may be surprised and delighted at the abundance you attract.

Money as energy in motion

No matter what your relationship to money is *now*, or how much you have, there is always room for change. If you haven't fully confronted your fears about money, then it's unlikely any circumstances, including a windfall, will relieve the fear. Is money *influencing* the way you feel, or is it *determining* the way you feel?

Perhaps you are refusing to face your fears about money? Maybe you are using the 'Ostrich System of Money Management' (OSMM) and sticking your head in the sand. It takes an enormous amount of energy to avoid confronting anything, and that's energy you are not directing elsewhere. If you are investing energy to *avoid* facing your fears then you don't have all your available energy to attract 'functional financial independence'.

Are you letting money *determine* your happiness? Handling money as an emotion begins simply, right now. If you are going through a time when things seem particularly scarce, sit and feel your anxiety and fear around money. Feel it to its extreme for about ten to fifteen minutes, then get on with your job. In this way you free up the energy you may have been avoiding in *not* confronting the emotion.

An acquaintance related a story to me recently that depicted how some people let money *determine* their emotions. She was sitting in a restaurant with two friends of hers who were in an intimate relationship. They were fighting and carrying on about this, that and the other, while sharing a meal because they couldn't afford a meal each. My acquaintance went to the toilet, and when she returned she witnessed a different scenario. Her friends were chatting amiably, and each was enjoying a desert. She asked them what had happened. They replied, 'Daryl just came in and returned the fifty bucks he owed us!'

Money as a behaviour

Money helps to influence the balance of power in relationships. Have you ever loaned money to someone who couldn't pay you back, or owed money to someone you couldn't pay back? An unequal relationship is established. This can certainly be the case when it comes to bills. It's disempowering to have bills we are unable to pay, or think we are unable to pay.

If you owe money for bills, remember this: *creditors can't eat you*. It's empowering to call creditors and say, 'It's my intention to pay, yet I'm unable to pay you now. What do you suggest?' It shows you are not avoiding them and are willing to take care of matters. This is money as a functional behaviour. You are taking responsibility for yourself and not living the OSMM.

How do we behave with money? How do we behave around others with money? How do others behave with us? In intimate relationships, the behaviour and conflicts triggered by money are often associated with separation and divorce. I read an article once that stated that 90 per cent of divorces involve money issues.

Many couples I have worked with over the years have said they successfully worked through more issues by looking at their awarenesses about money than they were able to in long-term counselling. In these situations, money seemed to have been the trigger for one person to feel 'less than' or 'more than' the other person. Where feelings of 'more than' or 'less than' existed, equality wasn't being expressed. The greater the level of equality between people, the greater is the capacity for intimacy between them.

If you have a partner, take time to talk about how each of you feels 'more than' or 'less than' the other around money (see the exercise in Chapter 8). Remember, it's *never* about the money. You might well be surprised at what comes up. The same goes with your business associate(s) if you have one or more.

What is money as a behaviour? In a business partnership it has the potential to cause strife and disagreement. When two partners are not in alignment about money, there's the potential for a nasty break-up. If you are employee rather than a partner, look at where you stand with your employer as far as money is concerned. Do you feel 'less than' because you are being paid 'less than' you feel you are worth?

Money as power, authority and control

I often see money used to exert power over others. Viewing money in this way is the result of learned behaviour. Many of us have felt, or, in fact, been controlled by money.

As kids we may have received pocket money for doing certain chores. This was part of our 'learning to earn'. Depending on how our parents presented money to us, it may have been used to control us. 'If you cut the grass, you will get your pocket money'; 'If you don't wash the car, you won't receive your pocket money'.

We can help kids develop a functional as opposed to a dysfunctional relationship with money by giving it to them when they do these chores, *as well as* giving them a weekly amount that is not reliant on anything. Even if they are misbehaving, they still get the money; it's unconditional! In this way, they don't learn that money is solely based on reward and punishment.

As adults we often feel controlled by money, too. This is often illustrated by our feelings towards banks. A bank can frequently represent unresolved family issues around power. After all, banks hold our money, they charge us for keeping it there, pay us a pittance in interest, make us stand in line and, to add insult to injury, sometimes charge us to put money into them! This makes us feel disempowered and controlled.

These feelings have intensified over the years as electronic banking has become increasingly 'popular'. ATMs are preferred by banks to bank employees. While some people actually like this, there are others who bemoan the loss of that personal touch – a real live human being to interact with.

The 7-day weekend

If you want to balance the scales in the banking stakes, then consider a credit union, or *shop* for a bank. I wanted to open a new account so I took several hours to 'shop' seven banks. I looked for a particular attitude; for banks that knew they were in business for *people*. I asked questions about bank charges and loan policies. One thing most people don't think of when they want to borrow money is to ask the banker how to get money from their bank. Shop around. Bank staff are actually paid to help you do this.

If you are considering taking out a bank loan for your new right livelihood, meet with the loan officer or bank manager of different banks and note who is responsive to your queries, who goes the extra mile to be helpful, and who reflects the attitude you want. Shop banks like you would shop car lots if you were looking to purchase a vehicle. Banks can be great teachers. We can know we have healed many of our power, authority and control issues when we stop whingeing about them.

One of my mentors, Jim, decided he wanted to buy a bank. He dropped out of school at age thirteen and was a millionaire by age thirty. He found a little bank in Arkansas and went there to see what he could do. When he returned we were sitting on the edge of our seats waiting for Jim to tell us he had bought the bank. In his southern drawl he said, 'I bet ya'll thought I bought that bank? Well, I didn't buy that bank. I went down there and I said, "Shoot, if I'm the largest single depositor in this little ol' bank, I'll run the show anyway and don't need to fool with the rest of the stuff".'

He took a huge chunk of money and put it into this very small bank. He didn't need to be on the board of trustees. He didn't need to handle everything from bank charters with the state to meetings with the federal reserve board. Yet, pretty much whatever he said, went. This shows you don't need to own to have control. You don't need to be a millionaire either. Take a look at where it might benefit you to control – not own.

Money as a pattern

I've defined a pattern as an 'unconscious repetitive behaviour'. How much of your money life fits this definition? Are you using the OSMM?

Keep a personal spending record for ninety days. When was the last time you categorised each area of expenditure, that is, food, rent, entertainment, taxes, electricity, phone bills, clothing, travel, household items, etc.? You may not like what you see, yet it will move you towards 'functional abundance', that is, sound fiscal management. That is the freedom that comes from clarity. You are now dealing with the situation as it really is.

The financial deficit disorder simply means the fundamental lack of money. More accurately, it's the fundamental *feeling* of suffering from a lack of money and has little to do with the *amount* of money we have. It's a pattern many of us live; it seems to be epidemic in Western countries.

The chronic feeling of 'not having enough' extends much further than money itself. Feeling that money is scarce often has something else at its core; we know by now that it's *never* about the money. Sondra Ray, in her book *Loving Relationships*, talks about *personal laws* we observe. Two common unconscious beliefs are 'I can't get enough' and 'I'm not good enough'.

Let's imagine either of these personal laws as a rock. At the core the rock reads, 'I can't get enough' or 'I'm not good enough'. Attached to the rock are various floating balloons which represent money, time, sex, energy and love. The rock (an unconscious belief) affects the balloons (the different areas of life) by being at the core.

If your core says 'I can't get enough', no amount of money will suffice. If your personal law is 'I'm not good enough', you may never get the amount of money you want or, if you do, you may find some way to sabotage your financial success, or just continue to feel unfulfilled. To overcome your core personal laws you must first become conscious of your patterns. You can do this by clearly observing how you relate to money while you keep your ninety-day spending record.

Acting like eagles, thinking like buzzards

One of my mentors used to say that out of any random sampling of one hundred people, ninety-five are *thinking* and *acting* like who are scavengers feeding on dead prey and only five are *thinking* and *acting* like eagles who soar high above. And that's on a good day! It's a comment on their attitudes, not on the people themselves.

As we are growing up, environmental conditioning generally trains us to behave like sheep. It tries to box us in and keep us the 'same' as others. This breeds a tendency for buzzard thinking, that is, not rising above the crowd and owning your own magnificence.

It requires a certain strength to know we are all different and to be comfortable with our differences. Being different from the rest also involves certain risks. Yet, if we take these risks we develop eagle thinking, and enjoy a freedom that allows us to soar.

Our friends often have an investment in keeping our relationship with them exactly the way it is. When we begin to fly on our own, watch out. Are your relationships as they are now *really* supporting you and your hopes for joyful financial independence in whatever it is that you choose to do. Do they attempt to keep you in your comfort zone?

Once I heard someone ask the question, 'Where are you getting your financial advice from?' Are you getting your financial advice from a neighbour who is either unhappily employed or scraping along? Chances are, if your neighbour really knew about money they wouldn't be your neighbour. They'd be living 'up on the hill on their estate'. Choose carefully where you get your advice from, and be aware of that ol' buzzard thinking. Think like an eagle and you will fly.

Money as a habit

I've learned that a habit can either be made or broken in somewhere between twenty-one to twenty-eight days. Often our feelings about how much money we have (or don't have) can be simply a result of *habit*.

Exercise 1

By keeping a personal spending record you can begin to get clear on your financial position. After a month, total each category and show it as: a) a percentage of total expenses; and b) as a percentage of total income. For example, if your total expenses for the month are $2000 and you spend $500 on food, then food is 25 per cent of your total expenses. If you have $4000 coming in that month, then what you spend on food is 12.5 per cent of your income. (There is software on the market that has budgeting programs available, for example Quicken or MYOB.) Once you've done this you can make any necessary changes based on what your priorities really are. This is a good habit to get into because if you don't get clear on where you are now, you *will* wind up in a new place still carrying around your 'old baggage'.

Exercise 2

You may have picked up habits from your parents and others regarding money. A quick and simple method of determining what you have and haven't picked up from others, is to write a small paragraph about how Mum is/was with money, how

Dad is/was with money, how you are like Mum regarding money, and how you are like Dad regarding money. Acknowledge what worked for them and what is working for you. See what isn't working for you any longer and how much of it was learned from your parents. This gives you a sense of whose beliefs you are living.

Money as an attachment

Some of the greatest unhappiness around money happens because of our *attachment* to it. Lots of millionaires are unhappy because they are *attached* to their money and what it represents. However, 'functional millionaireship' has a minimum of attachment to money itself.

During the crash of 1987, a millionaire relative told me it was the first time since he had been in business that he was having trouble collecting from his largest accounts. I asked him, 'What's going to happen if the bottom falls out?' He replied with a chuckle, 'I guess I'll just be out there with the rest of them.' Clearly he didn't intend to be 'out there with the rest of them', clearly he was concerned about his account receivables; yet it was also clear that he didn't really have an attachment. He had learned from the 'failure' of a previous business that attachment can cause distress, dysfunction, damage and disorder.

In creating our right livelihood we can do our best, surround ourselves with capable professionals and employ effective systems, and still have no control over unforseen economic situations.

However, we can be *committed* to our right livelihood and yet not *attached* to the results of it. Attachment can trigger anything ranging from mild anxiety to severe emotional suffering. Remember: we are only responsible for our actions, *never* the results.

Do what you love and the money will follow

This is the title of the bestselling book by Marsha Sinetar. When I say, 'Let money follow your passion', initially everyone I say it to gulps a bit. Some even think it's ridiculous.

In my trainings with others, I take it one step further. I ask people to pick a financial goal that is two- to two-and-a-half-times greater than their highest annual net income in the past. I find many people achieve this goal once they are living their right livelihood, even though at first they can't imagine it could be possible. It's simply too far removed from their present reality.

A lot of your resistance to the 'cliff jump' and showing up in the world in all your exquisite glory, may be the fear that financially you'll end up in the toilet. My experience has shown that just the opposite is true.

Jerry Gillies wrote a book called *Moneylove*, a wonderful book on the similarities between love and money. Love is a primary moving force in our lives. It therefore stands to reason that if we are expressing more of our love for ourselves in the work world, then the work world will return that love to us multiplied in the form of money.

Reverend Ike is an outrageous black minister from Harlem in New York City. He rides in 'mile-long' limousines and loves helping people live their prosperity. He is committed to people and says in essence, 'Live the life I lead. I'm not taking your money to spend on a limousine, I want you to spend your money on driving a limousine that is even longer if that's what you want. You can go to the ocean with a bucket or a spoon. The ocean doesn't care.'

In your financial life are you going to the ocean with a bucket or a spoon? Do you feel worthy enough to let the shower of abundance rain upon you while saying, 'Thank you, thank you, thank you, thank you'?

This is not greed, folks. We are not coveting what we are receiving, we are simply seeing it as part of the universal flow. People often quote the Bible as reading, 'Money is the root of all evil.' It actually reads, 'The *love* of money is the root of all evil.' It's *never* about the money.

The cornucopia of true 'financial abundance' is not 'out there'. It's *in you*. You can experience the abundance you see in nature. Keep a green tree in your heart and perhaps the singing bird will come.

Chapter 5
A Timely Affair

> *'If you want something done, give it to a busy person.'* – common expression

I often say to people, 'Time is the most valuable thing you have.' Sometimes the response is, 'What about health?' To this I say, 'If we don't put any *time* into our health then we ain't gonna have much health.'

We often take time for granted. It just *is*. When you are creating your right livelihood, learning about time is 'of the essence', particularly if you want to be self-employed.

Most of us know what it's like to be told by an employer what *time* to be at work. We are also told what time to have morning tea, what time to have lunch, what time to have afternoon tea, and what time to go home. At work we are usually conscious of keeping our 'eye on the time', or thinking 'time is flying', 'time is dragging' or 'I'm running out of time'.

When people say, 'It's time to go to work', this is usually the time every one *else* is going to work and what we get is – you guessed it – peak hour traffic! Many progressive employers now have swing shifts which allow employees to avoid rush hour traffic. Some employees are now able to work at home thanks to technology. Avoiding travel to and from work can be a huge time saver. Regardless of your employment situation there are two things to keep in mind about time. First, how you are *valuing* your time and, second, how you are *using* your time.

Valuing our time

How *are* you valuing your time? Generally, how much we value our time is commensurate with our level of what we feel we deserve and our own self-worth. It's like the old adage, 'If you bargain with life for a penny, then life gives you a penny in return.' Also, we usually organise, plan and prioritise our time in direct relationship to how we value it. We all have 168 hours in a week. What are you doing with yours?

As we grow in life and develop a greater sense of self-worth we typically value our time more. There are a couple of ways to increase the value of your time. One way is to continue personal development work in whatever form this may take: counselling, reading and listening to self-help literature and tapes, and therapy... the list is long. This will help you achieve a clearer sense of self. Self-awareness is clearly an ongoing process and is as much a journey as it is a destination. The other way to increase the value of your time is to be paid (or pay yourself) more, which can often produce startling and immediate results.

Personal growth work usually involves changing our *beliefs*, which in turn attracts a new set of life *experiences* to us and becomes our new *reality*. This is cause and effect. This is reflected in my own experience of having worked with various forms of therapy for a number of years. I worked on my conditioning, and that fundamentally revealed my personal belief which said, 'I'm not good enough'.

I worked with various types of processes to rummage around the vast warehouse of my 'biographical sketch' to find out where I had learned to feel less than worthy. When I was able to get in touch with the patterns, beliefs and behaviours that fed my feeling of 'I'm not good enough', I could begin to let them go. This was a process and it *did* increase my level of what I felt I deserved and my self-worth.

You can go directly to changing your *reality*, and then you attract a new set of *experiences*. This ultimately results in you changing your *beliefs*. This is what is called effect and cause. The combination of *cause and effect* and *effect and cause* can be potent.

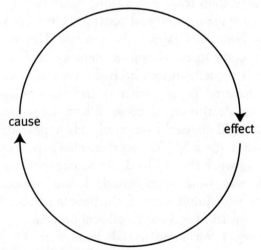

- change = awareness + action
- money as energy, habit, emotion, behaviour and abstraction

Years ago I experienced this directly when I was first starting out in marketing and consulting. My fee was $30 an hour. I was new at it all and eager. I approached just about anybody who would listen to me. Quite frankly, I didn't have much self-worth at the time. I attracted a number of Ma-and-Pa-type operations – people who didn't really understand me or what I was doing. As a result of their limited budgets and limited knowledge of marketing management, I helped them develop some seriously limited marketing programs. I found they rarely implemented my suggestions.

They also sensed my low self-esteem. Because I was such a 'people pleaser', I would give them three hours of my time and talent, and bill them for only an hour. I also found that I had a tough time collecting my fees. I was effectively earning $10 an hour, working with people I felt I was wasting my creativity on, and spending too much time being a bill collector. All the while some part of me was saying, 'You deserve more than this.' Then along came Nate!

Nate gave me my first real contract. Unbeknown to me at the time, Nate was fabulously wealthy. He owned banks, insurance companies, shopping centres and a publishing company. It turned out he also had an a vocation: finding as yet undiscovered people with talent and giving them an opportunity. As the saying goes, 'When the student is ready, the teacher will appear.' I was ready. He appeared.

Nate gave me a $1500 contract, plus expenses, for doing ten hours of work that I loved. An amazing thing happened. My *work* was now appreciated, I was appreciated, my suggestions were implemented, the people I worked with were 'fun to play with', I was paid well and on time.

However, I felt some initial discomfort. My feelings of lack of deservedness were amplified and I wasn't sure I was 'good enough'. Then the magic began to happen. Some time into the third or fourth hour of this contract, I began to start feeling worthy. My reality changed; I attracted a different set of experiences and, lo and behold, my beliefs changed.

At this point I began to believe my time was truly valuable. After all, it was being valued by others who were successful, in my opinion. My experience with Nate was a powerful shortcut. No matter what feelings or emotions were churning inside me before, when I met him and was given this opportunity, something changed. I increased my feelings of deservedness and started to prosper from this relationship. After working with him I attracted clients similar to him: no more unappreciative, whingeing, difficult ones.

Hanging out with others who value *their* time can teach you a great lesson and give you a feeling of joy, freedom, satisfaction and accomplishment. Who are you hanging out with? What are you doing with your 168 hours a week? Are you *using* it wisely?

Using your time wisely

There was a time in my life when I was doing all the *right* therapies, workshops and seminars, striving to find an undefinable level of deservedness and self-worth. I believed when I finally 'found' this level of self-worth *then* I would be more successful. I revelled in the fact that I was diligently collecting insights and awarenesses about myself. Yet, these somehow seemed to 'fortify' me against the need to take the appropriate actions. I felt action would trigger fear, frustration, and other feelings and emotions that would ultimately culminate in failure.

It took me a number of years to come to an understanding of my attachment – and, occasionally, addiction – to my personal development work. I'm not discounting the accuracy of my self-knowledge attained during my personal development work. I simply know, in retrospect, that without attaining the additional self-knowledge that only comes through actual experience, it had serious limitations. It was important for me to take my awarenesses – to the streets – and *fear forward*.

I learned a great deal about using time being by being in relationships with people and having clients who didn't value their own time. They have been (and are) some of my most valued teachers, as I learned they didn't value *my* time. I allowed them to, in effect, determine what I was going to do with my time. Some of the ways I let them do this included adjusting my daily schedule to accommodate people who were chronically late. On days I planned to be finished work at 5 pm, I often left at 7 pm – all the while keeping people who were on time waiting. This wasn't working for me any longer.

Again, Nate helped me move past this. I wasn't seriously late for appointments – just late enough, often enough. Nate was a man who valued his time and used it effectively. He was patient with my behaviour for a while. Then, one day, after a series of gentle requests and suggestions, he said, 'Your consistent lateness shows me that perhaps you have an inflated sense of self-importance.' I looked at him with a combination of bewilderment and shock. My initial thought to myself was, 'There's no need to kill a housefly with a cricket bat.' He then said, 'What you are really saying, Stefan, is that if *you* are important enough to *me*, I will wait.'

I had never thought about it that way. This was an incredible piece of learning, and the shock helped me to learn quickly. It had a particular impact because I held Nate in such high esteem and had such great respect for him.

You know something? I was never late for an appointment with him, and rarely late for any appointments with anyone else, at any time thereafter.

There's no excuse, perhaps other than **resistance to leaving the familiar,** for not learning how to use your time functionally, effectively and wisely. When you achieve this you will discover greater freedom. No planning book, calendar or time management course will teach you anything unless you take action and develop the habits that these systems suggest.

In my personal consultancy practice, I finally got to the point where I would make it very clear that if someone had booked a one-hour session beginning at 2 pm, then the clock would start running at 2 pm whether they were there or not. At 3 pm, that was it; the hour was up and they would pay for the whole hour. It wasn't easy at first, as I felt I was being rigid and unsympathetic, yet over time it became second nature. I was able to communicate effectively with others about how I used my time. Inherent in this was the act of conveying how I valued my time. I never told anyone how to use *their* time; I simply got clear on how I wanted to use mine. The rest was up to them.

Over time, I observed a couple of things. I noticed the people who were chronically late and *really* wanted to work (and play) with me somehow found a way to be on time (would you believe, even doctors!). I know people who are still chronically late for everybody else and on time for me. At the same time, I found I was attracting more and more people who used their time like I did. Today, I rarely have last-minute cancellations. Everybody knows I request and require twenty-four hours notice. If I don't get it, and it's not an emergency, or an act of God, then it may be months before they can get in to see me again.

Prioritise

An important part of using time well is prioritising.

Take a moment to define and describe the priorities in your life (as they stand now); this process will support you in expressing your right livelihood. First, you may want to get clear (or clearer) on what it is you *don't* want to be doing. Short-term, intermediate and long-term plans will give you form in which to express your function. The function is to say, '*Yes*' to the life you want. Begin now by prioritising each day, and perhaps each hour.

Plan

Professional Human Being Gina Pronesti said, 'Plan like you're going to live forever and live like you're going to die tomorrow.'

A year is an interesting composite of cycles, seasons, months, weeks, days and hours. Did you ever notice how fast they go by and, as the years pass, how the speed seems to increase? Then you die. On your death bed will you be wondering, 'Why didn't I ... ?', 'What if I had ...?' Will life be something that happened to you while you were busy doing other things? Will you be so caught up in the activities of life that you forget to plan what you *really* want to do? A farmer plants crops in advance, a developer plans projects in advance, fashion designers plan their upcoming lines, cities plan for the future (believe it or not), couples plan to get married ... the list is endless.

If you're not clear on planning, go to the library, visit a bookshop, take a seminar, talk to friends who are successful planners, buy planning books, and get a sense and a feeling for the whole process of planning. The next year is made up of 365 boxes. As the Chinese say, 'The journey of 1000 miles begins with the first step.' Your next year begins with the next day. Make it a priority. Plan what you want to do with it.

Depend only on dependable people

I now depend only on dependable people. There was a time when I felt everyone was letting me down. I could not count on people to do certain things at set times, or even show up on time. It seemed like an 'undependability' epidemic was happening.

The first and most natural place I went to look was within myself. Here I dug deep and uncovered a place in me I wasn't able to depend on. I discovered I wasn't relying on my intuition, or the feelings I was feeling. I wasn't listening to my heart. As a consequence of this it became obvious to me why I was attracting people I couldn't depend on.

Then I began a search for what the word 'dependable' meant to me. To me, dependable smacked of dependency and it was during that phase of my life that I was experiencing the anti-dependence swing of the 'interdependency' pendulum. No longer in the extreme of co-dependency, I was not yet at some kind of *interdependent* balance. We can use every situation, occurrence, and relationship in our daily lives as an opportunity to learn and grow. Eternal vigilance is the key to a life of creative self-expression.

When I began to unearth the fossils of my environmental conditioning and re-experience and release a host of childhood disappointments, I was able to see my relationship with time and people more clearly. I confronted the residuals of broken childhood promises, shattered dreams and betrayed trust. I realised the feelings of anger, being controlled, resentment and futility that were aroused when other people 'let me down' were just what I needed in order to change my *reaction* to other people's use of their time. As an educator, I began to see the futility of teaching others how I wanted *them* to use *their* time. It was like peeing in the ocean attempting to make the tide come up.

I also couldn't subscribe to the 'If you can't fight them, join them' mentality. I'd already walked a mile in their moccasins and was unwilling to regress. I chose instead to attract people who valued and used their time the way I wanted to value and use mine. Even though I am an educator, I am also a student. I made the decision to hang out with the 'big kids' who had what I wanted. They valued and used their time creatively, productively and joyously. I worked with the affirmation, 'I depend only on dependable people.' I did my lines – seventy of them – every day for seven days.

It's a funny thing, commonsense! It is so *un*common. I was determined to do it *my* way and fly like an eagle. Trading in my 'buzzard' relationship to time with an 'eagle' relationship to time made perfect sense to me. Simple? Yes. Easy? It can be if you know you are using and valuing your time in a way that no longer suits you.

Write down the names of the people with whom you are in a regular, ongoing, relationship – be it personal, social, or work – with a comment next to each name on how they value and use their time. What results do they seem to be producing? Do they produce these results effortlessly? Are they balanced in their use of time? Do they exhibit a balance with family, recreation, entertainment, and work? Now acknowledge the relationships that are working for you. Consider changing the ones that no longer serve you.

The three Cs

When you are evaluating the way others value and make use of time in relationship to you, take note of courtesy, consideration, and commonsense.

- Courtesy is letting others know if we are going to be late.
- Consideration is having respect for others' time. Rescheduling may be an option.
- Commonsense is simply recognising how others value their time. If you're working with someone who is always on time, respect that. On the other hand, if you have a doctor's appointment and are running ten to fifteen minutes late, chances are the doctor's behind time anyway – have you noticed?

Time to dream

Time is the most valuable commodity we have. The more you live the beauty of your dreams, the more appreciation you will have for using your time effectively. You'll have more things that you enjoy doing and even more you want to share. You'll have time to play more, learn more, live more and love more. Begin now to value your time in a way that embraces *having it all*.

Chapter 6
Creativity — It's More Than Arts and Crafts

> 'Creativity comes only from discontent.'
> – Krishnamurti

I use this quote from Krishnamurti in workshops. People sometimes react to the word 'discontent'. Yet it need not denote gloom and doom. Discontent, in this context, can mean something as simple as wanting to shift the position of your body as you read this book. It may mean opening an umbrella because it has started to rain – or it may result in writing a letter to the council. Feelings of discontent can inspire us to make change. In our lifework we may be ready to make change simply because we are 'sick and tired of being sick and tired'.

In Nature, when eagles build a nest for their young, they line it with thorny branches and then lay soft straw or hay over the top. When their chicks are old enough to search for their own food and it's time for them to be independent, Mama eagle throws the soft bits out of the nest. The young eagles feel the spikey branches and are compelled to leave the nest and go on to their greater good.

When we feel discontent we can be inspired to create something new and fly off to greener pastures. We may paint another painting, dance a different dance, compose a new arrangement, wash the car, clean the house, go to the beach, or create our passionate, sizzling, heart-centred, joyous right livelihood!

Suzy had an artistic flair and loved to play around with calligraphy. She would send letters to friends and family with addresses exquisitely written on the envelope. People began to ask Suzy if she would address envelopes for wedding invitations and other special events. She accepted because it was fun. When she went in search of suitable cards, none of them captured the special uniqueness of her clients and their events. So, soon, people were asking Suzy if she could write in the cards as well as on the envelopes. That's when she started to experiment. She began to design her own cards and write her own poetry. She researched the market and noticed there was nothing out there like she was doing, and her business 'Creativity Unlimited' was born. For many years now, Suzy's company has been designing and marketing unique handmade cards tailored specifically to people's desires and requirements. Her 'discontent' gave birth to a highly creative and successful venture.

Creativity unlimited

We often think of creativity in relation to arts and crafts, and other obvious expressions of creativity such as music, writing, film making, and the like. Let's expand our view of creativity and see that it can embrace *everything*. When we look around with this mindset, we see everyone and everything as a grand and glorious expression of Infinite Creativity.

When it comes to our right livelihood, we can see creativity expressed in the way we relate to others and in the way we bring our dream into reality. The way in which we assemble the pieces of our 'passionate puzzle' is creative. In other words, you make up your own dots and connect them any way you want.

The extent to which we can expand our experience to embrace the notion that everything we do is creative, is often the extent to which we can express our joy in our lifework. What we are speaking of is a creative journey. We express our vision and create our own destiny using our *internal* compass and we make our *life* an adventure, not simply a career. Life and everything we do in it is creative.

In school I took a creative writing course and thought it was a rather strange course title. I had always viewed writing, in all its various forms, as creative. It didn't hurt to have a Mum who had been a journalist, either.

A friend of mine recently started one of these writing courses. She would leave heartbroken after every lesson. She thought she wasn't 'creative' enough to be a writer. She ploughed through her discontent and soon a new realisation emerged. She discovered she had been *judging* her creativity. Of course she was creative. It was *her* work, no one else had written it! *She* had created it. Let's leave the judgements to the critics – that's their job, and even *they* are simply expressing *their* opinion.

Separating our creativity into little boxes (painting here, gardening there) is one of the greatest obstacles to living a fully creative life. It's easy to recognise creativity in certain

Creativity — It's More Than Arts and Crafts

areas of our life. Why then don't we see creativity in the way we use our time, the way we dress, the way we express ourselves, the way we cook, the way we clean our house? The list is endless (another endless list!).

In my work with people and, indeed, with this book, it's my intention to stretch people's imagination and by doing so challenge their creativity. T.S. Eliot wrote, 'Only by risking going too far, can you find out how far you can go.'

Consider practising this three-day experiment. Remind yourself, beginning in the morning, and then throughout the day for three days, that everything you are thinking, doing, feeling, and saying is *creative*.

The Buddha said, 'We have 50,000 thoughts a day so we have 50,000 opportunities a day for enlightenment.' I say, 'We have 50,000 opportunities a day to recognise and express our creativity.' We can see it in ways we may not have thought of in the past.

At the end of the third day write, record, compose, paint, talk, walk... do whatever, in celebration and recognition of the heightened awareness of your creativity. Be as imaginative as you can with this. Have a 'creative' party or a 'creative' bath.

If you don't already have a mental picture of what you would love to be doing in your right livelihood, there's a major opportunity here to stretch your imagination. What do you want to be doing? As mentioned in the first chapter, one way to be clear about your goals is to make a list of ten things you enjoy doing most in your life — things that are not necessarily work-related.

In the West, we are 'form-challenged'. We are attached to the form of things and often miss the function. We take the myriad colours of our personal rainbow and attempt to squeeze them into the the typical job description which

leaves out an extraordinary part of who we really are. When you design your right livelihood from the ground up, you set the foundation with activities that put a smile on your face, which is a *highly* creative process.

I was standing outside my publisher's office in downtown Sydney watching people scurry around to move their cars every hour to avoid the possibility of receiving a ridiculously exorbitant penalty. Actually, it's less like a penalty and more like a punishment. I did a bit of mental time-lapse photography. I saw a dozen or so cars parked on the street and their owners running in and out to move them every hour. As I 'fast forwarded' this scene in my mind, not only was it hilarious, it also gave birth to a creatively inspired opportunity.

I thought, 'If there are a dozen cars parked on this one street, there are probably fifty parked around that one block, all in one-hour parking zones.' I had this idea that for five dollars a day one or two people could move these cars for their owners. They'd carry a mobile phone with them in case anyone wanted to leave or get in touch with them. At $5 per car, per day, that's $250 a day for one block. Within seconds my creative thinking expanded to include scores of similar city blocks. In a matter of moments, a very prosperous idea for a small business was born. Doing the sums on just ten blocks came to over $600,000 a year. It beats working at McDonalds!

Each of us miss more opportunities in a single day than we can take advantage of in a lifetime. The source of creative inspiration is limitless, and there's no shortage of ideas to implement them. Whoever came up with the hoola hoop, the pet rock, the frisbee or the slinky? They are simple, creative, fun ways to play – not to mention the financial independence they gave their inventors. Didn't Benjamin Franklin discover electricity by flying a kite?

Accept your creativity

When your creativity and emotions are attuned, you can go anywhere you wish to go in life. Your creativity can feed you and keep you warm. Holding judgements that say you must *work* at being creative keep you from expressing your creativity in all areas of your life. Releasing limitations allows you to really enjoy yourself without working at something you don't want to do. Judgements that do not allow you to do what you want to do need to be released. Judgements create beliefs which, in turn, create your *reality*.

Limited notions of creativity do not allow you to assess a situation for what it is. Creativity born of these limitations isn't able to grow. We also tend to overlook the opportunities available for expressing our creativity. Begin now to see where you have been holding other people's ideas and beliefs about what creativity is. Release them and let your true (present) feelings tell you more about your *real* creative self.

Also, you can release feelings that suggest you do not deserve to express your creativity. Comparing your creativity with that of others doesn't work either. By doing so, you are not being open to what is appropriate for *you*. Get in touch with your heart. Let your heart show you that you *can* recognise your creativity. You will know because it will *feel* perfect for you. Finding your own unique creativity will be reflected in your outer reality.

We have been taught (well) that gifts are a reward for dedication and hard work. This is another judgement, and releasing it is necessary, too. If we do not, it sets us up for struggle. Contrary to popular belief, when you succeed in releasing the notion of hard work and struggle, you are able to express your creativity effortlessly and easily. Your creativity is *yours*, no one else's. The idea is to allow *your* creativity to evolve and to succeed. To do this it is necessary for you to accept that you are creative.

Creative listening

Listen for your creative desires. Clear the space to hear. How have you been denying your creativity? Have you been denying you have it, telling yourself it's somehow not good enough, that it's not time? Fine tune your inner listening skills. Express your creativity without *any* thought of the results. Listen, as you create a conversation; watch, as you drive creatively in traffic; see yourself create as you dress.

Start now to release any judgements you have about creativity. Begin to accept that you are a result of Creation. Reclaim that part of you which knows that *who you are* and *what you do* are the same. Stretch your creative vision to include expressions of joy and limitless abundance. Let the limitations on your creative self vaporise. Allow your creativity to soar and deepen your experience of life.

Creative energies

Matter is neither created nor destroyed, merely changed from one form to another. *All* exists in the Universe and all is available to us to manifest on a 'material' level through creative intention, commitment, focus, specificity, perseverance, and the willingness to do whatever it takes *no matter what*.

If I were to bring into existence a new business moving people's cars hourly around downtown Sydney, I would have fun assembling the pieces and seeing what else evolved from this adventure, such as car cleaning, taking them in for maintenance and registration, lunch delivery, and who knows what else! I'll bet you have some ideas. By the way, you can use this one. I have an unlimited source of them. I'd be interested to know if one of you 'eagles' runs with this. If you do, you can send me a tithe!

When I had that creative flash for the 'car-moving' business, I also felt a moment of excitement and exhilaration which, interestingly enough, no one around me seemed to share. I believe no one shared my excitement because they knew I wasn't going to follow through with it. It probably sounded a bit far-fetched and they were experiencing a little unconscious jealousy, or, perhaps, all they could see were the so called 'problems' associated with the venture. How often have you seen or felt this happening during times of change or while 'creating'?

All my life I've heard, in response to my ideas – 'It's not done that way. You can't do that. If it was worth anything it would have already been done.' – and a host of other similar responses you may have experienced yourself. All of these statements say 'no' to the infinite nature of our unique creativity.

Have you ever watched a child find a hole for a square peg? They first attempt to put the square peg in the round hole. When it doesn't fit, they put it in the triangle hole. The child keeps experimenting with other shapes until they find the square hole. It is a highly creative process. I sometimes watch with amazement the *patience* and *perseverance* of these littlies. Can you find the child *in you* and remember those times of seemingly endless play?

Have you ever noticed that when you are doing something you *really* enjoy how effortless and easy it is and how time flies? How much energy you have available and how satisfied you feel? The real voyage of discovering the passion in your lifework consists not just in seeking new lands, it's also in seeing with new eyes. If you want the river of your creative life to flow smoothly, start today and create a new ending.

In creating the next step of your right livelihood, you have an opportunity to sit playfully on the seashore of your creativity, building the sandcastles of your dreams. Are the sandcastles of your dreams sky high? Great! That's where they start. Perhaps it's time to pull them in like you would a kite. Dare to create the beauty of your dreams in your lifework.

Chapter 7
Emotional Self-Mastery

'Discussion is an exchange of knowledge; argument an exchange of emotion.' – Robert Quillen

Have you ever felt flat, empty, or a lack of energy? During childhood most of us learn to shut down emotionally and so we may miss out on truly enjoying a vital aspect of our make-up. The personality includes physical, mental *and* emotional components. While each of these is related and inter-related, each has its own subtle differences. Rather than allow our emotions full scope, we usually shut them down, though we can never shut them out. The energy we use to suppress, repress, reject, displace, judge and deny our emotions moves to the upper centres, especially the mind. It's like a garden hose with a hole in it. If you shut off the nozzle, the spray from the hole increases.

As children, we were encouraged to develop certain mental faculties. We learned early to value intelligence, memory, reasoning, logic, and other functions of the mind. All the while we received scant attention or encouragement in developing and mastering our emotions. Mostly we just received judgement and punishment for their expression.

There's a memory course infomercial (often seen on TV during the early hours of the morning) where the 'memory man' remembers and repeats the names of everyone in the large audience after each person says their name only once. My response to this feat is, 'What a waste.' While people are impressed when I remember their names, I also have no problem with asking someone to please tell me their name again.

That leaves me wondering if much of the energy invested in developing various functions of the mind, such as memory recall, are not undertaken at the expense of developing a well-rounded and balanced personality: a personality where the physical, emotional and mental are operating together in harmony. I mean, really folks, what's the use of being able to remember fifty people's names in a room? Surely it's more important to be able to *recognise*, *accept*, and *appropriately express* my feelings and emotions?

Recognising your emotions

Have you ever noticed someone giggling at something when you know they are angry? Many of us have conditioned responses that stop us from feeling the *real* emotion we are experiencing. How often have we felt agitation, which is a rather innocuous feeling, only to recognise, when we take time, that underneath it is anger, or sadness, or fear, or some other emotion.

We *can* recognise emotions if we take a moment to breathe deeply and get in touch with what is happening in

Emotional Self-Mastery

our body. It's also important to recognise that our behaviour is propelled and motivated by certain emotions. We've all had days where there seems to be so much to do and so little time, where things don't feel as if they are getting done. This triggers agitation. If we can recognise our feelings and emotions and take a break from what we are doing – even if it's five minutes in the toilet at work – chances are the job will be more easily and effectively completed.

Accepting our emotions

Accepting the feelings and emotions we have become aware of means not judging, blaming or criticising them. The conventional view is that feelings and emotions are caused by specific events, situations or people. We often witness this in our use of language. We may say, 'He made me so angry', 'The traffic aggravated me', 'Margaret made me late'. These and hundreds of other similar phrases involve judging, blaming, and criticising something or someone 'out there'.

The trick here is to 'unhook' the emotion from the trigger and take responsibility for how we feel and then choose how we will respond.

We can begin this process by being conscious of how we communicate our feelings, and how we can express our feelings more accurately, such as, 'I felt angry when he threw the dishcloth at me', 'I was feeling aggravated while driving in peak hour traffic', 'I was late because I didn't leave Margaret's place on time.' These and similar ways of using language allow us to take personal responsibility for the full range of feelings and emotions we may encounter in any given situation.

In most cases, *we are never angry at that which we think we are angry about.* If we are honest with ourselves, we may find our anger is triggered simply because we can't have *what* we want, *when* we want it, in the *way* we want it.

When experiencing grief, keep in mind that grief is the emotion of completion. On the emotional level it may even be the completion of something that happened to us long ago and has been forgotten: perhaps a spanking when we were four.

Accept your emotions and let them evolve in a loving way rather than a punitive, non-accepting or unloving way. When 'all of you' comes into loving acceptance of your full range of feelings and emotions, your life cannot fail to come into alignment with your dreams.

Expressing emotions appropriately

Appropriately expressing our emotions is often most challenging because of accumulated beliefs. In the process of growing up, we learn it is not appropriate to express the full range of our emotions. In fact, people are sometimes locked away in institutions because they have been diagnosed as having certain behaviours considered to be 'unacceptable'. In some cases they were releasing their suppressed emotions. When our emotions are severely repressed, this will often lead to an explosion of violence, resulting in serious harm to both life and property. Appropriately expressing our emotions is best done in private, whether it be in the privacy of our car, our own home, or out in nature. Begin by expressing your emotions, even if it's for only three minutes at a time, in a place where you feel safe. Learn to express your emotions appropriately and free up your energy. In this way you'll be able to direct it where you really want it to go. As Carl Jung said, 'The only way out is through...'

When I travel into the city, I leave the car and take the bus. I remember one particular day coming into the city to work on this book and having a hard time getting the words to flow. There was also a cacophony of noises in the busy publishing office that were distracting me. It was a very *long*

Emotional Self-Mastery

day, and by the time I had finished I was feeling a great deal of agitation. I was loathing the prospect of taking my already 'delicate condition' home in peak hour traffic on public transport. Given this scenario, it came as no surprise that the bus I ended up on was populated with the most annoying characters I had ever seen. When the bus pulled up at my stop, I flew out the door as if I was being chased by a lion.

My first thought was to head straight to the pub across the road. The other was to go back to my place and do a bit of emotional 'work'. It wasn't much of a challenge for me to recognise and accept that I was feeling anger. When I got back home I closed the windows, turned up the music, took the pillow and started pounding on the bed. After a few minutes, I took a some deep breaths, had a big glass of water and took a shower. Guess what? That stuff from the day felt like ancient history and I could enjoy the rest of the evening. The process didn't take more than twenty minutes.

There are many ways of feeling better. You could attempt to pray it away, meditate it away, run it away, walk it away or exercise it away, yet there are no substitutes for 'going through' and fully experiencing the emotion. It is usually the fastest way to do it and the most effective.

You cannot beat your life into the appropriate shape. Accept life exactly as it is now and it will evolve gently and be in alignment with all of who you are. Maybe you *think* you have been holding it all together and are able to make it look good. If you're feeling frustration and don't seem to get the understanding and results you want, do more work on your emotions. Recognise, accept and express them appropriately.

Emotional healing

Does it really serve me to have a highly developed mind if, when I'm driving in rush hour traffic, I transform into Attila the Road Rager? I'd rather not be so smart. Instead, I'd like to express more love, joy and laughter in my life. What we are striving for is to express success in life on all levels with grace, harmony and balance. I don't know of any thorough way that this can be done without acknowledging the importance of healing and evolving the emotions – believe me, I've done a fair bit of research!

We are developing the quality of success that embraces *all* of who we are. As we move into our right livelihood, we actually make a change in paradigms. We are moving from separation and departmentalisation to wholeness and unity. Enjoying our right livelihood gives us an opportunity for emotional healing. When we learn to recognise, accept, and express our emotions appropriately; we learn we are not our emotions, we simply have them. How often do we say, 'I am angry', 'I am happy', 'I am hurt', rather than 'I am feeling anger', 'I am feeling happiness', 'I am feeling pain'? When we use language in this way, we get in the habit of seeing feelings and emotions as a part of us, rather than all of us.

Feelings and emotions can often dominate the psyche to the extent that we are not conscious of our mental and physical aspects. When we feel our emotions we think that is all there is, letting them take us on a rollercoaster ride – especially the biggies such as grief, anger, rage, terror and fear.

How do you handle grief?

Grief is an emotion we have all experienced. We express grief at the loss of a relationship, the death of someone close, or when a child leaves home. Grief is *extreme* sadness. In the past, it was not OK for Western men in particular to express grief. Instead we have been conditioned to 'hold it all together and make it look good'. When we look at the big picture, men have ultimately failed in 'holding it all together and making it look good'. Thanks to the 'men's movement',

Emotional Self-Mastery

we have come to a greater understanding of our emotions. Men are beginning to allow themselves to feel, trust and appropriately express the whole range of emotions.

Grief is the emotion of completion. We all know how to complete a project or situation mentally. When we allow the full free expression of this feeling, we are able to 'complete' our sense grief on an emotional level. Suppressed grief invariably surfaces at some point, often unexpectedly. This emotion can be displaced, transferred, or projected onto a person or situation when the original circumstances have long been forgotten. Unexpressed grief remains with us, affecting our lives in many ways. To effectively develop your right livelihood, emotional completion is necessary. We want to be keenly aware of not taking our old baggage with us, and some expression of grief-release would be valuable in enabling us to leave it behind. One of the most powerful emotional completions worldwide that I've seen was triggered by the deaths of Princess Diana and, a week later, Mother Teresa. We saw grief expressed globally. It was a form of planetary cleansing and allowed billions of individuals to express grief that had long been held in place.

One process to express grief is simple and effective. Once a day for three days create for yourself a safe environment. The best place is one where you won't be disturbed, or have thoughts of disturbing others. Have with you a timer, i.e. a kitchen timer, and say to yourself, 'I'm going to take the next twenty minutes to get in touch with, and express, my grief.' You may be feeling grief before you start the timer. If not, bring to mind a situation, event or song to trigger the emotion. Call on whatever you consider to be 'guidance' and let it rip.

Grief isn't necessarily attached to a specific event; it's rather the accumulation of a lifetime of situations, perhaps beginning with birth when we left the womb.

When the timer goes off at the end of twenty minutes, have a drink of water, regain your composure, and get on with

the rest of your day. There is one exception – and the choice is up to you. If you tap into a deep well of grief that doesn't want to be bound by a twenty-minute time limit, let it continue. You will know if this is appropriate. If not, you may like to visit a professional counsellor to help you cope with deep grief.

When we first start working with emotions there is always a fear. The fear is if we fully express our emotions, then we are going to somehow lose it and go off the deep end. The egg timer provides parameters so we know there is a beginning, a middle and an end to this process, and that these feelings are not going to continue forever. It takes an *enormous* amount of energy to avoid *anything*, and this is energy we are not directing elsewhere. In taking twenty minutes or so to express your emotions, you are freeing up twenty-three hours and forty minutes in the rest of your day. You will have more available energy for mental clarity, creative expression and physical health and wellbeing.

Let's take, for example, a fire hose attached to a fire hydrant. You can use this energy constructively to put out a fire. You can also take this same hose, point it at someone, and knock them over. Then again, maybe you want to tie a knot in this fire hose and watch it explode? It's the same energy, just different ways of using it. What emotions are, where they come from, where they fit, what to do with them, and how to express them, present some of life's biggest mysteries and challenges. 'Whatever we *resist*, will *persist*.'

Anger – the 'biggie'

Anger is often denied, displaced, transferred, projected, avoided, or anaesthetised. When it is finally expressed it erupts and is projected onto others or us for something we *did* or *didn't* do. It is usually triggered by some *action* or *behaviour*– or lack of it.

As I've mentioned, few of us have experienced functional family models showing others taking responsibility for their anger. It usually isn't expressed appropriately and is instead *dumped* onto others. The suppression and denial of this one emotion have wreaked havoc on this planet for millennia. Crusades, wars, lynchings, torture and punishment, murders and assaults have all been the result of our dysfunctional relationship to this one particular emotion, and our inability to recognise, accept and express it appropriately. In order to heal and evolve the emotion of anger, we each have a responsibility for dealing with our anger. Clearly it involves work, courage, commitment and time and can be one of the most difficult tasks in becoming fully human. Dealing with our anger may also provide some of the greatest gifts and blessings possible, i.e. more peace, harmony, wholeness, and love. There's an old Chinese proverb that reads, 'If you are patient in one moment of anger, you will escape a hundred days of sorrow.'

Mastering our emotions

All the factors of our conditioning – family, community, society, culture – would have us walk in the world with all of its foibles like Barbie and Ken dolls: with perennial smiles, eternal generosity and unyielding gracefulness.

Emotional self-mastery doesn't mean being emotionless. It doesn't mean being emotionally selective, expressing only love, joy, happiness and peace. We must also learn to recognise, accept and appropriately express anger, hate, rage, terror, fear and anxiety in a way that is healing. In this way, it harms no one and helps us to grow. Any work you choose to do on the emotions produces results, energy and forward motion, sometimes totally out of proportion with the time and effort invested. The return can be ten-fold.

The power inherent in mastering the emotions will show up in your increased effectiveness and productivity. You will also notice changes in decision-making and creativity. Your life will take on a new balance. Developing a deeper understanding of your emotions enhances the 'whole' person and gives gifts we never thought possible: greater physical health, energy, wellbeing, longevity, release of struggle, harmonious relationships, enhanced sexuality, financial independence and a lot more 'fun per hour'.

One of my teachers said, 'Those of us who came to live a peaceful life of total bliss will all be reincarnated as New York businessmen.' In other words, we came here for life lessons that speak of learning to be fully human. And that's human *being*, not human *doing*. We often forget when we are busy *having* and *doing* that there is a *being*.

Bend like a palm tree

Growing up with hurricanes in the sub-tropics, I observed that pine tree and oak tree branches break in a storm, yet rarely did I see that happen to a palm tree. They didn't break because they bent with the wind. We are 'bending with' our emotions when we recognise them, accept them and express them appropriately.

This is living your life in *alignment* rather than in *control*, and it allows you to use your energy in alignment with all that is around you. I once had an Aikido sensei (teacher) who was 158 cms tall with the countenance of an innocent child. He used to say to me with extraordinary grace, gentleness, and genuinely from his heart, 'I do not wish to use *my* opinion against *your* opinion. I wish only to help you with your opinion.' And so he did. The stronger my 'opinions', the harder I hit the mat! He only helped me along.

When we are in alignment with our emotions; when all we do is in alignment with our emotions; and when all that we are, including our emotions, is in alignment with natural laws, then we can express our passion and purpose without struggle. A friend of mine from Spain says, 'Effort, sí. Struggle, no.'

Your number one priority

Having read this far, you have probably gathered that one of the priorities in developing your right livelihood is mastering the emotions. When we speak of 'mastering the emotions', we are not talking about *transcending* the emotions. For example, my definition of courage is not the *absence* of fear, rather the *mastery* of it – feeling the fear and powering forward.

I believe we all experience denial in some shape or form. Most of the feelings of denial we experience involve the emotions. When we can make healing our emotions a priority in our lives, then vast resources of energy that have been locked in and hidden will become available. Creativity can be unlocked by using emotions to motivate the creative process. You can begin now to avail yourself of all your incredible energy, no matter what your present job or situation. You *will* discover a cornucopia of unexpected gifts if you decide to accept this mission.

Healing and evolving the emotions allow us to live the vision of ourselves that says, 'I have it all.' Does it sound farfetched? Does it sound like an impossible job? Is it too much work? Does it have anything to do with creating your right livelihood? If you haven't had this kind of understanding of your emotions before, consider having it now. It's worth it. If it doesn't work you can always return to your old ways.

Emotional judgement

responses is the extent to which we haven't fully availed ourselves of the awesome power and creativity inherent in them. If you are judging your emotions, i.e. you think certain emotions are 'good', others 'bad', I invite you to stop *now*. Of course, it's easier said than done. Yet, if you are willing to put in the effort you will find a new freedom.

Experiencing unpleasantness because of what you are feeling in your lifework is not some kind of punishment. This discontent is only a response to what you have judged or denied. Your discomfort is the trigger that gets your attention. What you choose to do with it now is up to you. The good news is – you *are* ready. If you weren't, instead of reading this you might be reading the back of a cereal box!

Chapter 8
Intimate Relationships

> 'Every person who walks into your life is a teacher.'
> – Andrew Matthews from his book,
> *Follow Your Heart*

In my workshops, trainings and seminars, I find there is always great interest in how right livelihood can work harmoniously and abundantly within intimate relationships. Our relationship with ourselves is intimate to some degree or other. The level of intimacy we are able to feel with another will be in direct proportion to the degree of intimacy we have with ourselves.

Life evolves daily. In the same way, our intimate relationships are also evolving. Taking time every day to be with ourselves helps us to replenish, nourish and get to know ourselves. The quality of the time and energy we invest in ourselves allows us to bring even more to our loved one.

If you are single and really do want to create your *ideal loving relationship*, then begin with a study of your relationship with yourself. You can't give anything to another that you don't have for yourself. For example, if someone asks you for a dollar and you haven't got a dollar, you can't give it to them. It's the same with love. If someone asks you to love them and you don't love yourself, then you can't give them love. You may act in a loving fashion; yet this is not the same as expressing 'love'.

If you look at yourself and say, 'My finances aren't working. My career isn't working. My physical health isn't working', and so on, then it's probably not yet time to create your ideal loving relationship with another. Often, what we call a 'relationship' is in reality merely an 'involvement'.

'Special' relationships

We may meet someone and after a few movies, candlelit dinners, and long interesting phone conversations, we then ask ourselves, 'Am I in a relationship?' More often than not, we are not in a relationship; we are in an involvement. Involvements often turn into 'entanglements' and, as mentioned in Chapter Two, an entanglement is 'that from which escape is difficult'. This is what we call 'special' relationships.

Often each person in a 'special' relationship will look at themselves and feel like 'fifty cents'. When they come together with another they think that will make a 'dollar'. You meet someone and it's like *some enchanted evening*, then you attempt to fit each other into the models in your minds of a successful relationship. What happens as a result is you don't end up with a dollar, you end up feeling like twenty-five

Intimate Relationships

cents because you take away from rather than empower each other. You *think* your relationship is a huge success in the beginning, then come the little annoyances which at first were cute – he snores, she picks her teeth. Reality sets in.

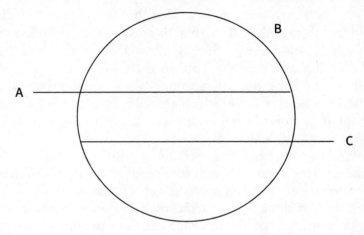

A: The Old Reality
B: The New Reality
C: Confusion

A 'special' relationship is one in which we look to 'someone' or 'something' to make us feel complete. This is impossible. No one, no object, no amount of money, not even our right livelihood, can *ever* make us feel complete. As long as we continue to sacrifice our *present* happiness for some *future* condition, then it is clear that we are feeling incomplete in the present. Our true power exists *only* in the present. If you are not feeling a reasonable amount of power now, in all areas of your life, it's unlikely you will feel it when you achieve something that you want, i.e. a dream relationship, right livelihood, more money. It is OK to have these things. What I am saying is begin *now* to develop a complete relationship with yourself. You are the only one who will *never* leave you. You are the only one who is *always* available to love you.

(W)holy relationships

If you are single and can say, 'Gee, my life is pretty much working' then perhaps it is time to open to the possibility of a (w)holy relationship. Simply know that at this point a relationship would be the *icing* on the cake. You know that without the icing you still *have* the cake – you are the cake! When you reach this point you are ready to attract a partner whose life is working in a similar way. You both feel complete and are ready to *have it all*.

Coming together consciously in this way allows for alchemy. This is very different from 'special' relationships that are often based solely on a strong initial attraction. What we have there is *chemistry*, not *alchemy*. If a relationship is based on alchemy, it's not about *finding* the right person; it's about *being* the right person. If you want to have your ideal loving relationship now, begin to develop a (w)holy (complete) relationship with yourself. Move away from judging, blaming and criticising, and towards a more loving acceptance of yourself, *especially* in those areas where you may feel incomplete and unlovable.

If you are already in a partnership and you want greater intimacy, then it's important for both people to know that their relationship is a vehicle they created so they could learn more about themselves. Relationship is one of the best workshops in town. There is nothing like a relationship to provide us with lessons and opportunities.

Ram Dass, a popular American guru, tells the story of a guy in a rowboat. He is rowing on a lake cloaked in a heavy, dense fog. He crashes into another rowboat and starts screaming profanities at the other 'person'. He soon finds out that the

other boat is empty! In a relationship the 'boat', the other person so to speak, is empty. A conscious relationship will acknowledge this. It gives us the opportunity to know that it is not about the *other* person. Instead we recognise, and accept, our personal responsibility in a growing relationship, as well as the grand and glorious opportunities and pleasures it can bring us.

Avoiding sabotage

In my work over the years, I have seen men and women use their so-called 'relationships' to sabotage their imminent success – or even take their recently acquired success and flush it down the loo. We can sabotage the next step of our success either by bringing in an inappropriate relationship, or bringing in an appropriate relationship at an inappropriate time. This isn't so much about personalities as it is about *energy*. No matter how much energy we have, there is still only so much available. We *are* human. During times of change and transition, a certain amount of energy is required to leave the familiar.

All new relationships go through a 'honeymoon' period. This can be a wonderful, giddy, romantic period of discovery and infatuation. It takes great discipline and focus to pursue our right livelihood at a time when a large part of ourselves wants to be with our new love as much as possible.

David was stuck in a dead-end job. He had been relieved of his managerial position, and continued working for the same company while keeping his managerial salary. He had been working in medical equipment sales for many years. He liked working in that field, yet felt his demotion had placed serious limitations on where he was going in the company. Over time the call for him to do something different amplified. He came to me for coaching.

David was single and when he started the training program I suggested he not invite a new relationship into his life until he was firmly grounded in his right livelihood. He agreed with the idea.

He worked for many months developing a functional relationship with his feelings and emotions, and completing many old beliefs and behaviours along the way. His physical health and wellbeing took a dramatic change for the better, and he found amazing new depths of creative expression. Fulfilling his passion as a writer, he sold his first articles to a national magazine, and soon after had a book of short stories published. He was on a roll. He started to get enquires from other publishers about doing a novel. Radio and television talk show requests were beginning to come in. He was feeling great, even though he had yet to sign a contract with a major publishing house, for the big one – his novel. It was at this point that David met Karen.

David described his initial meeting with Karen as 'electrifying' (that old chemistry thing again). Within a month they were 'totally in love'. Soon after, they moved in together. They both seemed to think this was logical and reasonable because Karen's lease on her flat had expired, and the owners were demolishing the building. She was also in between jobs, and didn't have any financial reserve. None of that mattered to Dave because it was 'hearts and flowers' time. He was going to assume the role of 'provider'.

I have nothing against romance. I am a bit of a romantic myself. Because of his preoccupation with his relationship, Dave stopped writing daily. He also footed the bill for all the household expenses because he was *feeling* his newfound wealth (although there wasn't much in the bank yet). Months went by and their involvement turned into an entanglement. Subsequently, they went their separate ways. It was at this point that he went back to work at a 'real' job.

Ultimately Dave got back on track. It took him another eighteen months. He is now firmly grounded in his new career as a writer. Remember, we learn through shock and repetition. Dave learned through a combination of both. There are many variations to this story. Make sure the relationship you want, or the relationship you have, is supporting you in creating your sizzling right livelihood.

If you are in a relationship now, invest the time and energy into communicating with each other about what's involved in the next step of your success. Make sure you are both in alignment when it comes to vision, purpose and finances. If you are not in alignment now these issues will surface later on, often in a way that has the potential to sabotage your dream. Develop a habit with your partner of asking for specific support and offering to give it in return. Change is a family affair. Recognise and honour the family dynamics and the shifts that can happen in your relationship with partners, children, friends, and associates as you move towards creating your right livelihood.

Equality in relationship

As I've mentioned earlier, it's important to have as much equality as possible in our intimate relationships. Intimacy is not to be confused with sexuality. Intimacy involves trust, communication, love and surrender, and is built over time. We all know it is possible to have sex without intimacy. We can also have intimacy without sex. To experience both in our ideal loving relationship is to *have it all*.

It's been commonly said, and effectively researched, that 'behind every great man is a great woman'. It's well documented that highly successful men usually have a great woman as a partner. I also say that 'behind every great woman is a great man'. As stereotypical roles continue to change in Western societies, we see more men become househusbands and full-time parents. In creating our right livelihood, we are witnessing major transformations in all types of relationships.

Larry and Stacey own their own retail business. Their life involves making business, as well as household, decisions together. When they came to me they found they were equally matched when it came to the running of day-to-day affairs. It was their relationship with money that seemed to seesaw. When it came to money, they rarely seemed to be on a level playing field. Stacey would sometimes feel 'less than' Larry when it came to money. At other times, she would feel 'more than' Larry. It was the same for Larry. They also had an implied agreement between them that there was 'never enough'. They were contemplating an expansion of their business and they realised their disagreements about money were increasing the closer it came to making the final decision. They came to me for coaching in order to reach another level in both their business relationship and intimate relationship.

I gave Larry and Stacey a Dyad (couple's exercise) and asked them to do it for eight minutes a day for the next week. I asked Stacey to say to Larry, 'One of the ways I feel "less than you" around money is...' Larry then said, 'Thank you', and nothing else. After two minutes (it's the egg timer deal again) they switched roles. Larry would then tell Stacey where he felt 'less than' her when it came to money. After two minutes, they would, in turn, tell the other where they felt 'more than' when it came to money. When the eight minutes was up they would hug if they wanted to.

After hugging they chose to have a discussion. They told me that some interesting things came up for them. They found out things about themselves and each other they never knew before. What Larry and Stacey found was that it was *never* about the money. It was really about where they felt 'inferior' or 'superior' in other areas of their relationship. Having had meaningful discussions about their thoughts, feelings, emotions and behaviours, Larry and Stacey were able to come to a new level of equality in a very short time.

As I've said before, the greater the level of equality, the greater the capacity for intimacy. Larry and Stacey experienced a new level of intimacy together. Not only did they express more joy and closeness with each other, they were also able finally to make the decision to expand their business. Their business went on to prosper as a result of their newfound closeness with each other.

Don't let others attempt to keep you in the familiar

You need to be aware of others' investment in keeping you in the familiar. The words and advice you hear are often well meant and intended. They offer support and encouragement, if not actual enthusiasm. The power of the subconscious keeps you in the familiar, and what is *really* going on may be quite different from what you are hearing.

Mark and Brian are mates who take the occasional fishing trip or family holiday together. They have been doing this since they were young. All of a sudden, Mark decided to leave his 'real' job and start his own business. It was an exciting journey. Over a period of five years Mark watched as his income doubled and then tripled. In celebration he decided to holiday in Paris with his family.

Brian has been a staunch supporter during Mark's transition. Yet while he is giving Mark encouragement, inside he is thinking Mark doesn't really need his encouragement because he has already 'made it'. Brian knows he can't join Mark in Paris because he can't afford to and he watches as Mark enjoys his new right livelihood. Brian is still stuck in the office where they first met, and is not ready to 'leave the familiar'. Although he appears to be full of encouragement, he also has an investment in keeping his relationship with Mark 'in the familiar'.

There are many variations of this story. Watch out for it. Be aware of those who may have a subconscious investment in keeping you in the familiar because *they* are not ready to leave *their* 'comfort zone'. I often see this in my personal coaching. One partner thinks it will be fabulous for the *other* because they believe the other needs help. When success and subsequent change occurs, I see attempts from the 'encouraging' partner to keep things the way they were. It can get v-e-r-r-r-y interesting.

If you look for your sizzling right livelihood to make you feel complete, it ain't going to happen. On the other hand when you recognise a (w)holy relationship with yourself, then you know you can *have it all*.

Chapter 9
More About Men — From Cro-Magnum to New Millennium

This chapter deals with the changing roles of men in relation to their work and life. Certainly, aspects of the traditional roles of men in Western society are being challenged. Not only are they being challenged, most men view this as a welcome challenge. It's a time in the history of the evolution of man when he is asking these questions more than ever before: Who am I? Where am I going? What am I doing here?

'Who am I?'

This is a question that many writers have addressed. Books by Sam Keen, Robert Bly, and others have increased in number over the years. The model of the good old bloke standing

The 7-day weekend

round the barbie with his beer, thinking about nuthin' more than fishin', sex, and a new boat still abounds, of course. They aren't reading these books – yet. It is a small and growing percentage of men that I am addressing.

Perhaps there are a few other residual questions lurking in contemporary man: those historical questions that have been a part of cellular memory from the Beginning. They were implanted somehow into the DNA and the chromosomes for men to unravel over a few million years of so-called evolution. Take a moment and think back. Remember when 'he' would leave the cave and go hunting with that big club? Can you see him in the latest designer fur outfit trudging out to secure dinner for the family? All of a sudden, there is his prey – a snaggle-toothed oxnard. He raises his chrome-tipped magnum club (this is where he got his name – Cro-Magnum man) and dispatches the beast forthwith. Another successful day at the office of Survival Industries!

Having put in a good day's work our man begins the commute home. Our dude always brings the 'office' home with him. That's his job, after all. Occasionally, his work comes home with him unexpectedly. This occurs when oxnards and other such animals decide to visit the cave dude and family unannounced and uninvited. Then he must swiftly use his chrome magnum to defend family, household, and perhaps even dinner cooking on the barbie.

OK, now we have a picture of what it was like then. Some might say that things haven't changed much. Of course, you and I are actually looking at what has changed and is changing so we won't dwell any more on Fred Flintstone, the chrome magnum man. There is another man that has evolved, and is evolving, from Fred. We've seen him over the centuries. He has tended to be more sensitive, more compassionate, more accepting, more creative and a lot more… While he has often gone to work at 'Survival Industries', he's done so primarily out of a need to protect and provide.

These twin needs to protect and provide traditionally have been stronger in the female of the species in most cultures. Could be that gene thing again. Nevertheless, we see our man evolving to a very different level. These guys have occasionally been called New Age Men. Instead of the animal fur outfit like Fred wore to work, our New Ager is attired in a blend of linen and cotton and real spiffy Deja shoes from California, made of 100 per cent recycled materials. This guy's so sensitive you almost wonder if he's in danger of imminent sainthood or something like that! By the way, I'm not convinced that there is anything 'new' about this or even that it is an 'age'.

My research and experience has always shown that out of the extremes comes the balance. Personally, my extremes ranged from my years as a self-centred, egotistical, arrogant macho male asshole to the period as an organic, warm fuzzy, recycled wimp! Ah, yes, balance and harmony works. Or rather the process of balance, for as we know it's in balance only until the next 'swing'. Having said all this, let me return to our main man here and his search for balance. Over time, we see societies and cultures finding the balance from the extremes as well as individuals.

Men, in general, don't have the role models for living life creatively and successfully based on their own definition of success. It's always been someone else's definition of success that defines their successes. Some commonly held symbols of success include amount of income, the car, the clothing, the vacations, the private schools and other definers ranging from the type of boat to the designer toothpaste. I say having all this is just dandy if we are not continuing to define ourselves simply and solely by what we have and do. The balance these men are seeking comes from a re-evaluation and realignment of values, priorities and lifestyle preceded by a time of extemes to whatever degree.

Lifestyle is as much an attitude as an organisation of material things. It's that grand experiment that a growing number of men around the world are exploring. It's the conscious and unconscious search for a way of being that reflects a way of having it all. This is what separates a lifetime of survival from a significant lifetime. I am not judging one as better than the other. We have lived a combination of both. For some men, this 'significant' way of living transplants the old way somewhere along the way. The shift can happen gradually over time. It can happen swiftly, triggered by intense situations and occurrences. With some men it can be a combination. Triggers can range from relational shifts and problems to loss of a job and income. Health challenges often contribute to these shifts in a profound way, as do sudden financial reversals.

Generally speaking, even the dramatic 'attention-getters' can experience early signs and symptoms. It depends on how much it takes to get us to notice that there's something happening. In other words, the intensity of a trigger mechanism is always equal to the intensity of the denial being held. A wee bit of denial and we might just lose a $5 note somewhere. A lot of of denial could get our attention by our losing our wallet and all the credit cards and money in it. As men grow, they find that life is less and less a random set of occurrences. Men are beginning to see the 'gestalt' of life. I see this as one of the biggest and most fundamental shifts I've observed in men in the last several decades. Men are, more and more, seeing the interconnectedness of all the 'different' areas of life. In the past, the greatest obstacle to a holistic and balanced vision of, and in, life has been man's departmental thinking. Perhaps that's part of a traditional tendency for man to use more of his left brain. That is the logical reasoning, sequential part. It may be that Fred Flintstone's Darwinian evolution embraces the use of his right brain more and more, all the while coming to a new balance and harmony in life and lifestyle. Go, Fred, go!

I really wonder who I am?

This is the question that Fred is asking himself these days. Evolving is not always so easy, he muses. Fred's thinking to himself that there is no longer the kind of certainty at work that he was accustomed to in the good old days. There was consistency and even a sense of awe during those times. Life at Bedrock Quarry was always dependable. Fred somehow always knew he would survive. Even if the Quarry shut, he could sit around and point in the sky and say 'whoa hot yellow!' That was a good job – not to mention hitting a tree with a rock – another dependable source of work.

What about now?

Fred is now in a brand new millennium – a 'state of the art millennium' to boot. An information age. A time of super highways that have super highways. Fred's adapted well. He has mastered the art of success according to contemporary definitions. These definitions range from his family to school and society. He's done well – very well, in fact. Fred's present-day Dino is actually a Ferrari and he's pretty much eliminated his old patterns of sabotage in his work world. Pebbles and Bam Bam are in private schools in Switzerland, doing well and enjoying themselves. Wilma still makes him feel like a king and he continues to adore her. Still, there's something missing for Fred. There's a growing sense of 'is this all there is?' The joy of 'Yabba Dabba Doo' is not the same either. Since his evolution as a man of the millennium, he's found gratitude, a growing sensitivity and a pioneering sense of 'what's next'! Truly, this is NOT the same old Fred from the old days. Yet, with all of this, here's Fred asking himself 'who am I?'

Fred is pretty typical of millions of 'new millennium' men asking this question. For aeons, man has found certainty, security, self-worth and identity from his work. Man has defined who he is by what he does. 'I do this, therefore I am.' Man and society have thought a person could be known from their occupation. Once upon a time, one's actual surname often came from one's occupation. Twenty years ago, I had some European-type calling cards made. They had an embossed border and my name elegantly printed in raised lettering. There was no mention of business. Often, when I handed them out, people would say, 'this doesn't say what you do' or words to that effect. To that, I would reply 'do you want to know what I do or would you rather know who I am?' Now that really got their attention! I guess I was making a statement to myself that what I did in the work world was not necessarily who I was.

New Millennium Man (NMM)

NMM is defining himself less by the various forms that his life takes and the labels for these forms. He is no longer satisfied to be known as 'butcher, baker or candlestick maker' and is finding other avenues to explore 'who am I?' – as a husband, a lover, a father, a man with emotions, a creative person, and the list goes on. NMM is asking himself how to assemble (or re-assemble) these various aspects of self into a unified, expressive, whole, healthy and happy person. He is also asking himself how to find these answers without much to go on from societal or family models. It's a kind of 'hunt and peck' type of search. While he doesn't want to feel as if he's reinventing the wheel, the fact remains that there is no blueprint available to him. NMM is ultimately on his own here with a bit of support from a few books and other men pioneering some 'maps' to refer to along the way.

Somewhere along the way, my own personal journey took a turn in the road. After 'living in the question' of 'who am I?' I began to observe some interesting dynamics. These included the realisation that the question 'who am I?' continued no matter how many answers I got – over and over and over again. I realised, one morning (almost literally), that the reward of seeking is more seeking! The perennial 'who am I?' continued to breed more 'who am I's?' So I decided that I would cease being a 'seeker' and start being a 'finder'. The day begins with the question 'what am I going to find today?' This is much simpler and, I believe, a natural next step for NMM.

Then the next question is 'what to do with what I've got': the daily application of the insights about who I am. Where am I going with all of this? For NMM, the process of transition is accelerating. From 'humble beginnings' of discontent come this growing confusion and feelings of needing to make changes.

Often it's not time to actually be making the changes he has in mind. You see, NMM is still learning to 'sit' with feelings and emotions, particularly during times of transition. It's all part of moving from the days of human 'doings' to the time of a new balance – the human 'being'. Man wants to take action as a way of not feeling all these feelings and emotions any more: the illusion that 'relief is just an action away', to paraphrase the antacid commercial.

All of this continues and makes daily life a challenge for NMM, especially the old Fred still in him who got a postgraduate degree in holding it all together and attempting to make it look good. NMM knows by now that he ultimately and always fails at both. It invariably falls apart and always looks shabby. Yet Fred Flintstone is still hanging in there as represented by the subconscious and its attempts to keep NMM in the familiar, in his so-called comfort zone. This is generally the time, individually and collectively, when NMM yearns for the good old days. Not really, he just wants some familiarity, some certainty and, indeed, some relief! Yet, he is past the point of no return. The biggest part of him couldn't return if he wanted to. Not really. You see, that's the way of evolution. That's the game. That's NMM.

Who am I? Where am I going? What am I doing here?

NMM wants congruity. He wants to live his life in alignment with his values. He wants to be able to recognise his Life Plan, the type of Life Plan that can help him know his purpose in life. He wants to live according to a growing vision that he has of himself and his relationship to his family, to his community and to his world. He wants to fulfil, in a more personal sense, his mission in life. He wants his right livelihood to include all of these. He is daunted by the loftiness of these tasks. He is confused about the how-tos of obtaining these goals. He questions his very worthiness to be entertaining such possibilities. He wonders where he can find support and how to support himself. All of this conspires to bring NMM to his knees in surrender. It is in that surrender that NMM finds his power. It is in that humility that he finds himself teachable. NMM finds his blueprint within. It's been there all along. NMM is the Phoenix that is arising out of the 'ashes' of dear old Fred Flintstone.

Perhaps you can hear it sometime – very late some still night when all is quiet. From the distance it comes like a celestial melody – a call from the Heavens. It is a divine balance of savage beat and angelic notes. It's the sound of the New Millennium Man celebrating. Listen ... *YABBA DABBA DO* ... *Yabba Dabba Do* ... *Yabba Dabba Do.*

Chapter 10
More About Women — From Wilma Flintstone to the Goddess

Actually, when you think about it, Wilma Flintstone was probably more evolved than we give her credit for. She seemed to have a sense of her own power. A confidence that allowed her to express her femininity and let Fred feel as if he was running the show. Of course, everyone knew who really was in charge, eh! So perhaps Wilma is not the best example of early woman. What about Ayla in *Clan of the Cave Bear*? If you're not familiar with the story (both as a novel and movie), Ayla was subjugated to the whim and the will of early man. As was the custom, Ayla was forced to live, as woman did then, subservient to the male. The story shows Ayla rebelling and making a statement that she was going to be powerful – and she did succeed.

More About Women – From Wilma Flintstone to the Goddess

As with man, woman historically fulfilled traditional roles in society. These roles included bearing children and being responsible for their upbringing. Other traditional roles have included being primarily responsible for householding. This is the job that does everything from caring for food to caring for the home itself. Certainly, back then, it was relatively simple (although not necessarily easy). She would take the animal that man would hunt and cook it. While he was out hunting, she would care for the children, keep the cave tidy and hope he would return. Because of the dangers, he would not always return. There was the possibility too that he would not return in one piece. No matter how well they planned their home, there was always the chance that they would be visited by a curious or hungry creature. Then it was into defence mode, whatever form that took. Scary, too! Those wild oxnards could be a real pain.

Here was early woman. A unique combination of that feminine, nurturing soul and one who was tough enough to survive and protect her brood. Sociologically and culturally it's interesting to see that, in some ways, things haven't changed much! When we take the long view, it's possible to see that we've almost come full circle.

Looking back to woman in her historical roles, we begin to see changes similar to the ones we've seen in the roles that man has played. It's almost as if these two creatures have begun to trade places! Man is having a renaissance of sorts. He is beginning to allow himself the freedom of feeling and emotional expression. While he's still not equipped for childbirth, he is becoming a capable househusband. Women are working in the professional world earning high incomes while Dad, with pleasure, takes care of the house and kids. I wonder what our dear Fred Flintstone would say about that? I'm sure the boys at the Buffalo Bowling Club would have a few choice comments as well. The entire notion of survival, what it involves, and the forms it can take, seem to be in a process of major overhaul.

The trends are conclusively pointing to changes in how a woman wants to relate to her life to work. Roles and behaviours accepted as 'simply the way it is' are shifting. Women are saying, on one level or another, 'that's *not* just simply the way it is for me.' We are witnessing a growing discontent with women who want 'simply' to be all that they can be in the world. The books, articles, seminars and other information about this subject are voluminous. Woman, like, man, is asking the same questions: Who am I? Where am I going? What am I doing here? Where's the map to guide women in the early chapters of the New Millennium? Is there a map at all? Is this another one of those 'make it up as I go along' deals? Could be. One thing that seems to put women in better shape than their male counterpart is her fundamental relationship to their feelings and intuition. While man is making that shift through trial and error, woman has typically trusted that intuitive part of herself more than man. It may very well be that this *is* her map.

The traditional institutions are disintegrating before us. The typical roles and relationships associated with men and women have served their purpose and are now being revised. While it is true that change creates opposition in the beginning, the tide continues to move along. For instance, the institution of marriage in the 'old days' was originally to provide equal responsibility in child rearing. Obviously, it stopped doing that long, long ago. Then there has been the good old 'till death do us part' covenant. That's a product of religion and the church. Particularly odious to many modern women is the 'obey' part of the marriage ceremony. These days, that's being traded in for words that speak about equality in a relationship.

More About Women – From Wilma Flintstone to the Goddess

The resistance to embracing a different, more contemporary form of relationship has fuelled a divorce rate of 50 per cent in the Western world. Now you can only imagine what percentage of those 50 per cent remaining together are unhappy. Staying in a tired, worn-out co-dependent relationship takes an enormous amount of energy. That's energy that woman cannot put elsewhere. Woman is rapidly awakening to this, and creating new realities for herself. This is often to the chagrin and dismay of partners, spouses, family and even friends. Woman is saying that she's proven herself as wife, mother, homemaker and it's time for more. It's time for a different experience. It's time to expand, to explore and to express. It's time for woman to be a mum and have a baby even without a father. It's a time when a lesbian or gay couple can parent a child. It's a time when women stay in school longer and graduate later; they are not in such a big hurry to 'partner and parent'. It's a time when woman and her partner defer parenting until later (if at all). These are the DINKS – Double Income No Kids. It's a time when woman is making cracks in, and in some cases, smashing, the 'glass ceiling'.

Woman, in the New Millennium, is infinitely better equipped than her predecessors. She has more education, more opportunity, and more support to live the beauty of her dreams. She's in better health, has more aliveness, and a deeper level of intention to get what she really wants from her right livelihood. She won't 'settle' for less. New Millennium Woman possesses a conviction of spirit to follow her inner voice. She is more patient. She knows that she needs to be, given the resistance of some men in the work world. NMW can be independent and self-sufficient without alienating the men in her life. She is a diplomat. The strength and courage that she feels at her core, helps her to accept and allow. She doesn't have a need to prove to others. She's not even sure she needs to prove anything to herself. She simply knows!

We hear about the 'glass ceiling' that affects women in business. This is the phrase used to define the limits of advancement. The perception of limitations for women, particularly in corporate situations, is changing. For many women the change is not fast enough. Yet it is happening. Women are making inroads into arenas that have traditionally been dominated by men. We are witnessing major shifts, particularly in banking and finance. Typically the domain of the male, women are asserting their abilities and capabilities in the world of money. Women are astute money managers, market analysts, financial advisers, share brokers and banking executives. Women have the talent for the decision making process. This includes a unique balance of left-brained logic and reason with right-brained intuitive and creative judgement.

I have worked with many women who can look at their 'jobs' in a very different way from men. Women seem to be more able to embrace the creative opportunities at work. Today's woman in business is more likely to recognise, evaluate and act on creative possibilities. Obviously, the 'glass ceiling' exists; however, it's being shattered more and more each year. I am also seeing that this 'ceiling' is being challenged in different areas. The publishing industry has been affected with more women reaching higher levels of success and climbing the corporate ladder. No longer are they limited to writing and editing, women are now running the show. Take a look at some mastheads of various publications. Find out where women are now – the President or CEO of the company.

When we observe enrolment figures at universities and business colleges, one thing stands out. The proportion of women taking courses and programs in business has increased dramatically. The number of female graduates with diplomas and certificates in marketing, management and finance has made quantum leaps in recent years. So has the number of women becoming lawyers and medical doctors. Complementary medicine has also seen a huge increase in female practitioners ranging from herbalists and naturopaths to chiropractors and osteopaths. Over the years, we have presented practice-development seminars helping people to employ systems for success. The average percentage of women in these groups has doubled in the last handful of years. Women want to know the elements of a successful practice and business. They are quick to grasp the need for systems and seem to apply them with a fair bit of agility. Women can understand the freedom that comes from using systems in their professional as well as personal lives.

The growing and obvious success of women as entrepreneurs is a powerful shift in Western society. Women are living the beauty of their dreams in ways that support the environment, contribute to humanity, model employee relations and produce profits. Women are giving themselves permission, if you will. One of my favourite examples is The Body Shop. Started in 1976 by Anita Roddick, this business has grown to over 1600 stores worldwide. The Body Shop has managed to embody all of the elements of successful entrepreneurship with a conscience. A percentage of profits are donated and, indeed, recycled. Villages in third world countries are working to produce product for sale through The Body Shops. Ecological mindfulness is also a hallmark of this business. Further, this business was one of the early, and strong, voices against animal testing of their products or ingredients. Anita, you've done well. Thank you.

The New Millennium Woman will continue to 'push the envelope' of success. The notion of male-dominated business and professions will be challenged at an even faster pace. Whether it be female astronauts, prime ministers, entrepreneurs, the numbers and influence will make quantum leaps. These changes will also increase in frequency in cultures and countries where women have been suppressed for ages. New Millennium Woman in these cultures will be able to show her face and hair in public – symptomatic of greater equality in all ways. Exciting times are upon us.

In creating her right livelihood, woman seems to have an easier go of it. She is able to grasp the concept that you can do what you love and the money will follow. She is a keen observer of the unhappiness that just working to survive creates. She sees it in men, particularly. She watches as the work-struggle takes its toll on men. Her 'study' of this begins with Dad. Here's the first man, generally, whom she loves and he's rarely around. He's gone most of the time because of this thing called work. She also notes, early on, that it makes him very unhappy. Perhaps it's this typical scenario that allows woman to better appreciate right livelihood: to embrace the possibilities of being in alignment with our passion and the power that ensues from expressing it in the world. New Millennium Woman understands that true success is when she lives her own life in her own way. This is not necessarily the 'Superwoman' or 'Supermum' we read about in the

More About Women – From Wilma Flintstone to the Goddess

Sunday newspaper magazines. NMW is not a human being able to 'leap tall buildings in a single bound'. She has found something else. This is more akin to living the congruity of a creative life of service fuelled by an inner passion.

It is this passion that propels her into new vistas and new definitions of success. NMW cannot, and will not, be dictated to any longer by the restrictions laid down for her in 'recent' millenniums. What's different now, also, is the way she goes about it. The time of the 70s, in Australia at least, was the decade of burning the bras. It was a time to demand. It was a time to get attention. It worked. The evolution has been pretty amazing. In just a quarter of a century, woman has managed to move from table-pounding dramatics – obviously necessary – to a different way of finding equality. NMW has completed the part that has felt the need to 'prove'. Now is the time to 'speak quietly and carry a big stick'. This 'big stick' is the energy that is being released as the result of releasing denial. It's the energy that is channelled by having all parts in alignment. It's the energy that is a component of the passion. It doesn't threaten most men and send them scurrying for cover any longer. The New Millennium Woman now goes about her business in a way that embraces man, allows man, and inspires him. She does her business in a way that includes man in a new partnership – a partnership of equality. Thanks Wilma, you've come a long way.

Chapter 11
The Only Way to Get Anywhere is to Leave Where You're at Now!

Well, isn't it? Let's have a closer look at the only thing in life that's permanent. Change. Yeah, we have no problem with the changes in the weather that Mother Nature brings. Sure we gripe and grumble about it sometimes – it's too hot, or too cold or too wet or too dry or too windy and so on. Basically, though, we accept the inevitable – that is, we really can't change the weather. Why is it then that when we experience change in life we often resist it kicking and screaming?

Somewhere, somehow, along the way we developed a model of life that doesn't support the life changes and

The Only Way to Get Anywhere is to Leave Where You're at Now!

passages that we go through. Sure, we see birth, maturation, middle age, old age and death as transitions. During times of accelerated change, it's easy to lose the plot. We are pulled along swiftly and usually we have a safety net! Inevitably, we are confronted with the knowledge that reality, as we've known it, is shifting right under our feet. Sometimes it shifts in a way that makes us feel we are standing in quicksand! These are the times when, perhaps, all that's left to do is to learn how to 'comfortably' free fall. There's not much that's familiar in our inner landscape and our ability to define it all becomes an exercise in futility. All the while, our subconscious is working overtime, attempting to keep us in the familiar – with limited success, I might add! Our exquisite subconscious is a potent and powerful part of us. Ah, yes, the subconscious has an awesome capacity to keep us in the 'comfort zone' (even though it may be fraught with discomfort). Of course, it's also the Motherlode! It is tapping into the subconscious to access the awesome power to have, to be, and to do.

Undoubtedly, you are reading this book because the 'shift is upon you'. Hopefully, these words can support you at this glorious time in your life. OK, so it doesn't feel glorious. You can take a moment here and now to celebrate the fact that you are taking the steps to put in place a plan. If it's too early for the plan here, at least you can know that the changes that are taking place are not unique to you. The way they are occurring is, obviously, uniquely your own.

Work, money and relationship are three of the most common trigger points for change. Yes, health challenges and crises also get our attention and accelerate that which has already been set in motion. You see, each of us has this Inner Plan that we came in with. It is not an add-on or an option. It is part of the original model. Sometimes, this Plan gets lost in the great shuffle of life. Learning to live this life successfully becomes a 'trial and error' sort of affair. Then, at various times, we happen across these so-called triggers to get our attention. It is at these 'moments' that we have an opportunity to have a closer look. It all sounds very step-by-step and logical. However, you know it can be anything other than logical and reasonable. Step right up, folks. We're talkin' 'bout life change in a way that rattles us right down to our boots. At least it can do so if we are considering the possibility of making fundamental changes in the way we want our life to work. So, here's a bit of a map that can be helpful in providing a context for your particular cycle.

This system speaks to what I call ages of development. It has its roots in an ancient Tibetan system. It has been roughly translated linguistically and also culturally. The latter so that the Western mind can comprehend it. As a student of cycles, I also see where this system complements other systems. The legend has seven, 7-year cycles starting at birth. The first seven years are the time for physical development. The second seven years are the time of emotional development. Then comes the time from 14 to 21 years. This is the time of mental development. From 21 to 28 is the time of spiritual and intuitional development. So, by the time we are 28, we pretty much have all the basic equipment. The cycle from 28 to 35, legend says, is the time to plan for the rest of one's life. In other words, that's the time when we first do our 'mum/dad' stuff. It's the time we work on core family conditioning. This happens whether we are 'conscious' of this happening or not. This time is followed by the age of development from 35 to 42. This translates into 'planning for the rest of one's life based on causes and effects of one's earlier life'. It's the time when we 'take it to the streets'. It's the time, not so much about 'who am I', rather the time of 'what do I do with what I've got', so to speak. Thirty-five to 42 is a time when we really learn to show up and put the previous learning

The Only Way to Get Anywhere is to Leave Where You're at Now!

into action. The auditions are pretty much complete. At age 42 you begin the next period of development. This is a time commonly labelled 'mid-life crises'. Needless to say, there is another more realistic way to look at it. Forty-two to 49 is a time, according to the legend, of 'learning to be at one with others'. It's a time, I say, when we act as if we had a 'PhD' in relationships of ALL kinds – that is, personal, family, professional and social. It's a time of learning discernment and discrimination on a deep level. Again, I say this happens whether we are mindful of it or not. It's no secret that I prefer that we understand what is happening. Then all this can happen with my 'permission' and the process of life learning can be extraordinary.

After seven 7-year cycles, guess what happens at 49? Ta-tum! Happy re-birthday! We are told that beginning at 49 we get to do it all over again, only this time we have the benefit of experience. We've done it once, and we get to do it again, which can be quite wonderful. For example, 49 to 56 corresponds to the period of birth to age 7 – the time of physical development. So any 'stuck' places, or crystallisations, in the physical body from the first seven years get an opportunity to be moved through the second time around. Wow! Certainly a different way of looking at the physical body. We can trade in the 'I'm getting old' paradigm. There are cultures that don't have the belief system of 'old'. Ageing is a grand and glorious time and in some cultures is actually accompanied by greater vitality!

The 'switch points' in this system are those median periods of moving from one cycle or age of development to another. Close to 90 per cent of our personal and professional coaching clients over the years point to these times of accelerated change as fruitful and important. These people are within a year either side of 21, 28, 35, 42, 49, 56 and so on. If you are in one of these groups, then you can validate yourself in one way. You're on the right track as far as having a predictable transition is concerned.

If you are not around a switch point year, look at your particular age of development for any clues that can support you in what's happening at this time. You can also do a bit of research. Have a look at others whom you've known for a time and observe where they fit into this system — or where the system fits into their life changes. The same activity, jobs, etc., at different times of life give us different life lessons. Variously, at different cycles we will also attract other activities, jobs, etc. for that same life lesson.

Whatever your age, you can now begin to utilise this magical system to help you see the opportunity for your life lesson. If you are in a transition age and feeling the effects of it, pause for a moment. Reflect on the seasons of the year. Imagine, for example, Spring. Spring has been called 'The Festival of Resurrection'. It is a chaotic time of many changes. It is a time when these little buds and blossoms and shoots spring forth. Spring is a bridge. Spring 'bridges' Winter and

The Only Way to Get Anywhere is to Leave Where You're at Now!

Summer. Using this Tibetan system, take a look at the 'Springtime' of your life.

Or is it the 'Autumn of Your Life'. Autumn has been termed the 'Festival of Transformation'. Let's dissect the word 'transformation'. 'Trans' means across. So it is the process of 'moving across form'. Autumn is the bridge 'transforming' Summer into Winter. It is another chaotic time. Like spring, the winds can howl and the temperature can swing widely in a single day. Whether you are doing your own personal Autumn or Spring, the point is the same – Chaos. Oh, sure let's throw some confusion into the stew just for 'fun'. Stir it all together and guess what? You've got yourself LIFECHANGE. Now, if you've had the kind of environmental conditioning most of us have had, you'd probably like your 'change of season' to be like this. You go to sleep one night. The sun set the day before at 5 pm and it was raining and cold – really cold – cold like two blankets, b-r-r-r-r cold! After a freezing night (of course you were cosy) you awoke to this scene. Ta tah! It's Summertime. Yeah. Time to put on your togs, grab the beach towel, and head to the water. Winter to Summer, just like that. Hello! Well, we know it just doesn't happen like that so why would we still hope for that type of change in our life?

Usually, the desire (subconscious, of course) to have it that way, or at least to want order and certainty, comes from a desire to be in control. We do this so as not to fully feel what's going on emotionally. Perhaps you've felt it 'enough' and it's time to move on. Does this fit? 'Surrender' is the same as giving up. It could be that I'm not 'good enough' to do this transition – 'right'. It could be just that old perfectionist impulse of not wanting to make a 'mistake'. Possibly, it's some combination of them. Maybe it's 'all of the above'. The thing here to remember is that your Inner Plan is always alive and well. You can't break it, you can't fix it, you can't get an 'A' in it, and neither can you flunk! The best you can do during this extraordinary time of change in you life is this: the best you can do. Embrace the Winds of Change.

It's quite possible that it's your Winter, or, perhaps, your Summer. Knowing which it is, is an 'inside' job. You will always know your season. Just stop 'pushing the river' and listen. You will know. Winter is the 'Festival of Identity'. It's the time when things come to know themselves. It's the season of maximum expression of inner creativity. Think about it. Underneath all that snow and illusion of dead branches, creativity is cookin' big time. Is it your Winter? Is it time to be still and reflect? Plan? Get Ready? You know if you listen carefully. Is it your Summer? Summer is the 'Festival of Manifestation'. The time of maximum expression of outer creativity. It doesn't require much of a stretch to get this one, eh? Yessiree, it's berry-picking time. Is it your Summer? Is it time for you to be out there? Showing up, expressing yourself, manifesting your creativity? You know. Listen carefully.

You are a person of all seasons. As you continue to allow your dreams to come into view, be still. Each season has a gift for you. A very special gift. A gift that no other season can give you. Relax. Take time to listen. What time is it for you now? The power that you want lives only in the present. It is your gift to yourself. A present, if you will. Sh-h-h-h. Listen.

In Closing

This book may or may not have been what you expected. Expectations aside, what has been presented here is a map. Of course, each of us has all the information necessary to get from where we are now to where we truly want to be.

What I've presented is not a collection of positive ways to recreate yourself. 'Positive thinking' is based on denial when it only focuses on one part of the mind. This part gets better and stronger while the other part is pushed further into denial. This may be why so many feel they must discipline, and otherwise pressure, themselves when it comes time for change. Your task now is to accept *everything* that exists around your present work, money, emotional, social, creative, physical and intimate life. Embrace your life exactly as it is *now*. By doing so you will reveal to yourself what it is you truly want.

Talk to yourself about your life now and make an inventory of your relationship to the various areas in your life. Accept your responses. Become aware of why your life has been the way it has been. Apologise and ask forgiveness where that is indicated. Celebrate your past victories, and acknowledge the exquisite lessons you've learned. Give thanks for the gifts and blessings that have brought you to this point – to this crossroads. In short, negotiate a new relationship with yourself. Release any judgements you may have had about your work, money, social, creative, physical and intimate life. Then allow *all* of you to participate fully in your life one day at a time. Develop a daily habit of celebrating *who* you are as well as *what* you do. Remember, you are a human being, not a human doing.

When you really start to explore this process, it may be ongoing for quite some time. Your outward reality will show you how you are progressing. Is your attitude to your present life changing? Are your relationships becoming more harmonious and more playful? Is that feeling of financial lack lifting? Do you feel more intimate with yourself? Is your body changing? Is there more energy available to you? Are you expressing more of your creativity in many different ways? Use these questions as virtual signposts. Use them to measure the results of your efforts. Your changing reality 'out there' will show you to what extent you are aligned with your essence. Regain your personal power a decision at a time, a thought at a time, a breath at a time!

Say yes! to your own 7-day weekend. The building blocks are perseverance, clear intention, commitment, focus, specificity and doing whatever it takes, *no matter what*! As you survey the raw material of your life now, you are able to recognise some powerful illusions you have learned in your life. The honesty and courage it takes is the stuff and

In Closing

substance of completion. Don't worry about new beginnings. Complete the past and you will attract your right livelihood in ways that may surprise you.

Have you been so overpowered by others and their beliefs and systems that you have somehow felt diminished? This has been happening for such a long time that many of us don't believe we have power over our own lives any more. Think of everything you have come to believe you must do just to be able to go on surviving in life. This is not the way it was meant to be for you. For others, perhaps. You – no! If that was so, you wouldn't be reading this book. Your recognition of your growing willingness to plan and prioritise your own life will increase your confidence and acceptance of yourself. Allow yourself time. What has been described here is simple. It is not necessarily easy. If you dedicate yourself to these suggestions you will begin to have feelings you didn't know you had. If your intent is strong, you will succeed.

You can use the development of your right livelihood as a way to transform yourself. Be clear about money and you will be clearer about everything else. Remember that it's *never* about the money! Learn about energy, patterns, beliefs, behaviours, feelings and emotions through your 'money mastery'. Use money mastery as an opportunity for mental self-mastery, non-attachment, and learning more about giving. The more you have, the more you can give. Give *yourself* the gift of giving.

Look carefully at the different parts of your life. Have you been seeing these components as separate from each other? If so, begin now to investigate your judgements. These judgements may have created the separations in your life. End all separations. The feeling of unity is a product of expressing all of yourself in all that you do. Find role models and hang out with them. Talk to others who wouldn't rather be doing anything else than what they are doing *right now*. Visualise and imagine being financially, creatively and emotionally rewarded for doing what you love. If you don't know yet what it is you love to do, begin by loving what it is you're doing now. The rest will follow.

I heard about an interesting piece of research. I was told that a survey in the United States showed that 80 per cent of people who start reading books of this kind don't go past the third chapter. If this is true, then you are part of the select 20 per cent who got to the end of the book. At any rate, you've probably gathered by now that creating your right livelihood is a metaphor. Yes, of course these pages were meant to clarify, support and motivate (if not inspire) you to find your 7-day weekend. The real message here is having *all* of your life working well. Creating your right livelihood, taking your passion to the marketplace and bringing your spiritual values into your lifework all give you the opportunity to soar like an eagle.

Anything unresolved in your life is *guaranteed* (and I make few guarantees) to come up around:

- The possibility of your right livelihood.
- The money thing.
- Perseverance, clear intention, commitment, focus, specificity and doing whatever it takes, *no matter what.*

If you realise and accept this as a part of who you are, you can move forward. This is where it can get sticky. You may sense that nothing short of *radical trust* will do it! **This is the 'cliff jump'.** This is the art of leaving the familiar. This is the point where the instructor finishes the fire-walking seminar, and you are now left to your own devices, while confronting your emotions, your bare feet, and a bed of scorching coals stretching four metres in front of you. Yes, you've been prepared. You know that others before you were successful. Does any of this eliminate your fears? No! So what's left?

In Closing

Action. 'Fearing Forward'. *'Feel the fear and do it anyway'*. I noticed the same thing each time I fire-walked: the coals were just as red and just as hot each and every time. 'Having the map' was helpful – yet it required action as well as awareness.

Is the information in this book simply going to become part of your accumulated knowledge? Or will you transcend this knowledge into wisdom through experience? Are you sighing with relief because all of this was too confronting and you're glad to finally be done with it? Did you nod your head in agreement with most of what was said and will you now put the book on the shelf or pass it along? Are you really ready for the Fire-walk or Cliff Jump?

'Oz didn't give nuthin' to the Tin Man that he didn't already have.' – The band America.

Let's take a lesson from the Wizard of Oz. The Tin Man got a watch. This was his testimonial. He was finally acknowledged. At last he got his *heart*. The Lion wished and wished for something that every other lion seemed to have. When he, at long last, got his medal he knew he had arrived. He found *courage*. The Strawman received his diploma after a very long search. Indeed, he was now able to *think*. Now, Dorothy looked and looked for power. She didn't know she always had it. *She* needed to be the one to realise it. Dorothy found the *dream* was in her own backyard!

Have you been looking 'out there' for your watches, medals, and diplomas to validate your mind, your courage, and your heart? Living the beauty of your dreams is an 'inside job'. Your dream is alive and well. Your dream is living in your own backyard!

Recommended Reading

Anderson, Nancy *Work With Passion*, Carroll and Graf Publishing, 1984.

Arrien, Angeles *The Four-Fold Way*, Harper, 1993.

Blanchard, Kenneth and Johnson, Spencer *One Minute Manager*, Willow Books, 1983.

Cameron, Julia *The Artist's Way*, Pan Books, 1995.

Chopra, Deepak *Creating Affluence*, New World Library, 1993.

Chopra, Deepak *The Seven Spiritual Laws of Success*, Bantam Press, 1996.

Clark, John *The Money or your Life: Reuniting Work and Joy*, Random House, 2000.

Covey, Stephen *First Things First*, Simon & Schuster, 1994.

Recommended Reading

Covey, Stephen *The Seven Habits of Highly Effective People*, The Business Library, 1989.

DeAngelis, Barbara *Confidence: Finding It and Living It*, Hay House, 1995.

Dyer, Wayne *Real Magic*, Harper Paperbacks, 1992.

Gawain, Shakti *Creating True Prosperity*, New World Library, 1997.

Gerber, Michael E *The E-Myth* (Republished as *The E-Myth Revisited*), Harper, 1995.

Gillies, Jerry *Moneylove*, M Evans and Company, 1978.

Hartley, Anne *Debt Free*, Doubleday, 1992.

Hartley, Anne *Financially Free*, Doubleday, 1990.

Hartley, Anne *The Psychology of Money*, Hart Publishing, 1995.

Hay, Louise *The Power Is Within You*, Specialist Publications, 1991.

Hill, Napoleon and Stone, W. Clement *Success Through a Positive Mental Attitude*, Thorsons, 1990.

Hill, Napoleon *Think and Grow Rich*, Wilshire Book Company, 1966.

Jampolsky, Gerald G. *Love is Letting Go of Fear*, Celestial Arts, 1988.

Jeffers, Susan *Feel The Fear and Do It Anyway*, Ballantine Books, 1988.

Kehoe, John *Money Success and You*, Zoetic Inc, 1991.

Mandino, Og *The Greatest Salesman in the World*, Bantam, 1985.

Mandino, Og *The Greatest Salesman in the World: Part II The End of the Story*, Bantam, 1989.

Peale, Norman Vincent *The New Art of Living*, Cedar, 1992.

Peale, Norman Vincent *The Power of Positive Thinking*, Cedar, 1990.

Ponder, Catherine *The Dynamic Laws of Prosperity*, DeVorss & Company, 1985.

Ray, Sondra *Loving Relationships*, Celestial Arts, 1980.

Roman, Sonaya and Packer, Duane *Creating Money: Keys to Abundance*, H J Kramer, 1988.

Ross, Ruth *Prospering Woman*, New World Library, 1982.

Sinetar, Marsha *Do What You Love, The Money Will Follow*, Dell Books, 1990.

Sisson, Colin *Your Right To Riches*, Total Press Ltd, 1986.

Sylver, Marshall *Passion, Profit, and Power*, Simon & Schuster, 1995.

Wilde, Stuart *The Trick To Money Is Having Some*, Hay House, 1989.